Outrageous Love, Transforming Power

How the Holy Spirit Shapes You into the Likeness of Christ

Terry Wardle

LEAFWOOD
PUBLISHERS

OUTRAGEOUS LOVE, TRANSFORMING POWER
Published by Leafwood Publishers
in co-operation with Sovereign World Ltd

Copyright © 2004 by Terry Wardle

ISBN 0-9748441-4-4
Printed in the United States of America

Cover design by CCD, www.ccdgroup.co.uk
Typeset by CRB Associates, Reepham, Norfolk

For information:
Leafwood Publishers, Siloam Springs, Arkansas
1-877-634-6004 (toll free)
www.leafwoodpublishers.com

To Sarah Herring –
a true servant of the healing Christ.

Other books by the author:

Exalt Him: Designing Dynamic Worship Services
One to One: A Practical Guide to Friendship Evangelism
Wounded: How to Find Strength and Inner Healing in Him
Draw Close to the Fire: Finding God in the Darkness
Whispers of Love in Seasons of Fear
The Soul's Journey to God's Embrace
Healing Care, Healing Prayer: Helping the Broken Find
    Wholeness in Christ
The Transforming Path: A Christ-Centered Approach to
    Spiritual Direction

Contents

Chapter 1

A Transformed Life

North American Christians are caught in a crisis of immaturity. Many would say that such a statement is unduly negative and merely my opinion. That may well be true. But it is a conclusion shaped by a quarter century of involvement in the Christian community as a pastor, seminary professor, and consultant to countless churches seeking spiritual renewal. More importantly, this immaturity is a reality that I have personally experienced and, sad to say, have contributed to professionally.

Countless churches are made up, and in many cases even led, by men and women who seem perpetually caught in spiritual infancy. Do these people believe in Jesus Christ as Savior and Lord? Yes. Have they learned the basic doctrines of the Christian faith? Probably. Could they give assent to the basic creeds of the Church, demonstrate proper Christian behavior, and point to ways in which they serve others in Jesus' name? I am sure that many people would pass these tests with ease. But my conclusion still stands. Christians are struggling with a crisis of spiritual immaturity, which is having a devastating effect upon their lives and the ministry of the gospel to a broken world.

The heart of the problem rests with the concept of Christian maturity. How that one issue is defined directly impacts the way in which a person seeks to grow and develop in the Christian experience. Many Christians, including local church leaders, think that being a mature Christian is relegated to believing the right things about Jesus and the faith, behaving like Jesus in daily living, and serving as Jesus did within the church and world. As such, a great deal of attention is given to knowing what to believe, how to behave properly, and where to get appropriately involved in Christian service. Sermons are preached, classes are taught, books are written, and ministries are formed to move people toward greater levels of understanding, action, and service. And, unfortunately, with this paradigm in place, maturity is measured by a person's movement toward this inappropriately defined end.

I realize that I must be very careful at this point. I do not want to leave the impression that belief, behavior, and service are unimportant to the Christian life. When properly understood, each plays a key role in a person's development. However, when these characteristics are the definition of Christian maturity, as is true in so many churches and countless Christian lives, there is a serious, even debilitating problem. Said more directly, Christian maturity is not measured by what a person believes, how he or she behaves, or the level of involvement in ministry. To do so only adds to the crisis of immaturity, causing people to give major attention to what is of less importance in Christian living.

The Call to Christian Maturity

I have known Jeremy for several years. He is the pastor of a small, but numerically growing church in the Mid-West. He is a seminary graduate, fine speaker, and innovative church leader. He has a keen understanding of theology, a good grip on the demands of ministry in a post-modern world, and a realistic plan for the ongoing development of his local congregation. Jeremy knows what he believes, is filled with integrity about the way he relates to others, and gives all he has in time and energy for the cause of Christ. And yet I am very concerned for Jeremy. I see that he, like so many other Christians, is caught in a crisis of immaturity. And, because he has bought into a belief, behavior, service definition of maturity, he doesn't even know what is wrong. But something is wrong at a very deep level, and it is crippling his life and his ministry. And it all relates to the issue I am addressing in this book. Jeremy does not truly understand the real call of the Christian faith, and as such, is investing in what is less important, just like countless other men and women who call themselves Christians.

What then is the true measure of Christian maturity? It is to become like Jesus. Do not be deceived by the seeming simplicity of this response, for it is packed with meaning and potential. This may be simply stated, but the concept is radical in its implications and demands far more and goes far deeper than belief, behavior, and service. Christians are to grow into Christ-likeness, allowing His life to mature within and be expressed throughout daily living. It is not just acting as Jesus would act, nor is it doing what Jesus would do. It is far greater than that. The goal of Christian maturity is expressed well by the Apostle Paul when he said, *"it is no longer I who live, but Christ lives in me"* (Galatians 2:20, NASB). Christians are to reflect Christ, growing to become more and more like Jesus all the time. Where Christian belief serves this end, it is being properly embraced. When behavior grows out of a person's true character, it is healthy and right. If service flows out of the heart of Christ alive within a person, then it is Kingdom empowered. Each of these investments can wonderfully serve the goal of maturing into Christ-likeness. But they only cripple development when they are seen as the shape of maturity, rather than serve as channels of the Holy Spirit's work toward a much greater goal.

Two questions demand immediate attention: "What does it mean to become like Jesus?" and "How does this maturation occur within the individual Christian life?" Both of these serve as the focal point of this book and are addressed here in an introductory and less detailed way.

What Does It Mean to Become Like Jesus?

I spent several months wrestling with the question, "What does it mean to become like Jesus?" I was motivated by my own desperate search for growth in Christ and a God-given concern for brothers and sisters locked in spiritual immaturity. I was, and still am, solidly convinced that there is more to being a believer than belief, behavior, and service. Christians are called to Christ-likeness. That process holds the power to impact lives profoundly, not just at the surface, but at the deepest level of personal existence. Christians who are empowered to grow toward that goal are unleashed into society as Kingdom people who can truly be salt and light to a broken world. They do this, not because it is what they are supposed to do, but because it is who they genuinely are in Christ. There is an authenticity that is irrepressible, causing other people not only to take notice, but be compelled to respond to the claims of the gospel.

Fully convinced that Scripture would give an answer that could serve as a definition of true Christian maturity, I turned to the Gospel record of Christ's life. From the very beginning I knew that the answer would have far more to do with the kind of person Jesus was than the things that He did in ministry, as important as those acts were. God's word did not fail to give up its treasure. I was soon able to see several foundational characteristics of Christ's life that must ultimately become increasingly true of every life that responds to the call to become like Jesus. These qualities and commitments, part of the very fabric of the Lord's existence, serve as the standard of Christian maturity for all. What was true of Him must increasingly become true of every Christian who wants to move toward spiritual maturity and wellbeing. The quality and characteristics essential to Christ-likeness are as follows:

The Characteristics of Christ

- Jesus rooted His identity in His position as God's Beloved Son
- Jesus experienced intimacy with the Heavenly Father
- Jesus was committed to community as a context for growth and ministry
- Jesus prioritized character above behavior
- Jesus responded properly to personal brokenness
- Jesus offered His wounds as a source of ministry to others
- Jesus was empowered in life by the Holy Spirit
- Jesus ministered with Kingdom authority

Christian maturity involves the issues of identity, intimacy, community, character, brokenness, ministry, empowerment and authority. Each of these Christ-like characteristics will be discussed in the chapters that follow. In each chapter I will look at the life of Christ as it relates to the stated topic, and then see what Scripture says regarding the concept with reference to every believer. It will become increasingly clear that growth in these areas is the essence of Christian maturation. As such these qualities should increasingly be the focal

point of our prayer, nurture, learning, and experience as
followers of Jesus.

Let me illustrate this point by returning to my earlier
discussion of Jeremy. As mentioned, he is a gifted man who
has a deep commitment to the Lord. He is also well trained
in ministry, capable as a leader, and effective as both pastor
and preacher. He knows how to divide the word of truth
rightly, behave as a Christian gentleman, and serve the Lord
Christ with effectiveness. But, as I stated earlier, Jeremy is
experiencing a deep crisis of immaturity. I know this
because I have spent a considerable amount of time with
Jeremy. There are foundational issues of Christ-likeness that
are not being addressed in his life.

Jesus rooted His identity in His position as God's son.
Jeremy has placed his identity in others and is wearing
himself out trying to please everyone. The Lord had an
intimate relationship with the Father, but Jeremy is so busy
in ministry that he seldom has time for such a relationship.
He also has no time to be part of a community of people
who genuinely care for him, though that too was part of
the Lord's life. Jeremy does work to behave properly, but
secretly struggles in defeat with impure thoughts and self-
gratification. He does not handle this brokenness well,
hiding it rather than dealing with it in a healthy way.

Jeremy does, by all appearances, have a good ministry, but
it does not flow from his wounds as it did from Jesus. Those
are also carefully concealed and left unaddressed, which
cause serious problems deep within Jeremy's life. Jeremy
understands the ministry of the Spirit and can teach about
power, yet admits that his own experience of infilling is less
than exciting. I am sure that was never a problem the Lord
faced. The Lord also amazed people with His authority. But
Jeremy, like so many who serve the Lord, struggles with
being taken seriously and often feels that even his best

sermons go unheard and unappreciated. As for priorities, well, I believe enough has already been said to show that Jeremy is often majoring in the minors. Jeremy does know what he believes, works to behave properly, and serves with all he has!

Is Jeremy a real person? Absolutely! The only thing false about this story is his name. Everything else I have said is true, a perfect example of the crisis of immaturity. And Jeremy is far from alone, for many believers struggle with Christian maturity. I developed an assessment question-naire aimed at identifying maturity levels among doctoral students at Ashland Theological Seminary, using the eight criteria described above. I asked three questions per characteristic and then added twenty other questions that focused more upon belief and ability in ministry. The responses were tabulated in order to find the mean response to each question.

The students, who were each involved in some level of full-time Christian ministry, scored consistently high in the area of belief and ability. They knew their theology and felt adequately equipped to do the work of ministry. However, the scores related to the eight characteristics of Christ-likeness were amazingly low. What stood out most were the responses that dealt with identity, intimacy, and com-munity. These gifted men and women were struggling significantly with their sense of identity, relationship with Christ in experiential intimacy, and commitment to growth in community. I shared the results with the students and it led to deep reflection, lengthy discussions, and serious times of prayer. They wanted these issues to be addressed in their lives.

While the results of the survey were negative regarding the characteristics of Christ-likeness, the response of the students was exciting to watch. Not only did they want to position themselves for this level of growth, they commented that they were hungry for the depth such spiritual maturity would bring to their lives. One student said that he had been growing increasingly dissatisfied with his Christian walk and now he knew why. What he hungered for was an authenticity of experience and relationship that he was not experiencing. He told the class that his previous approach to personal growth was an investment that was not paying any serious dividends in his life. But he now believed that the ache within his soul would be filled as he positioned himself for true growth and spiritual maturity.

Stated again, Christians in North America are caught in a crisis of immaturity. We may know what we believe about Christianity, understand how to behave appropriately, and commit to serve even sacrificially. But we are not maturing in the most important call of our lives, becoming like Jesus. And that goal, which is radical in both its implication and impact, must be intentionally embraced by leaders and laypeople alike. It is the call of the gospel, and holds the power not only to change lives, but change the world in the name of the One who has shown us what life is truly about as a child of God.

How Do We Mature into Christ-likeness?

What does it mean to mature in Christ-likeness? In the chapters that follow I will be identifying eight characteristics of Christ that should serve to define spiritual maturity. But first, it is critical to focus the discussion upon process. It is not enough to change the goal of maturity to these Christ-like qualities. There must also be a serious examination of the developmental journey. There too lies a serious problem. It would be easy to embrace the new focus of maturity, yet seek after it in the same ways as before by a performance-dominated effort at self-improvement. Many Christians, serious about their relationship with God, work hard to fulfill what they see to be the expectations of faith. They do this partly because it is what they are taught by Christian leaders. Pastors preach about what their people should believe, how they are to behave properly, and how they should serve the Lord. People then are admonished to get to work making all of this a reality. It is as if they are saved by Christ's grace, then must become sanctified by their own efforts. It does not work.

No amount of personal effort will change a person into the likeness of Christ. What people need is radical transformation, not strategies for self-improvement. They need a supernatural work that actually makes them new creations in Christ (2 Corinthians 5:17). There must transpire an act of God that miraculously changes men and women at the very core of their being. And that impossibility in human power is the good news of the gospel of Christ Jesus.

The Act of Transformation

The Apostle Paul wrote of this transformation in his letter to the church in Galatia. Paul was deeply concerned that the Galatian Christians were turning away from the gospel of Christ (Galatians 1:6). Apparently some people were telling them that being right with God involved far more than trusting in Christ. They were teaching that Christians had to obey certain religious laws to be truly righteous before God, adding to the message of the Gospel. Paul was irate. He told them that it was impossible to gain righteousness through rules. Had it been possible Jesus would not have needed to die (Galatians 2:15–16). But, as Paul taught, the law simply brought condemnation, showing everyone how far they were from the righteousness God required. Righteousness comes, according to Paul, by faith in Christ alone. At the end of that letter Paul emphasized this truth when he wrote,

> *"Neither circumcision nor uncircumcision means anything: what counts is a new creation."*   (Galatians 6:15)

When a person accepts Christ into his or her heart, the miracle of new birth occurs. The Holy Spirit places the seed of Christ's nature into the life of that believer and he or she becomes a new creation. Where previously the person reflected what was evil and broken in the world, now he or she has the potential increasingly to reflect the nature of Christ. What does that mean regarding spiritual maturity? The believer does not need to work at earning the character-istics of Christ-likeness, because the seed of that reality has already been placed deep within. Spiritual maturity is not something to be achieved by human effort, but received through the transforming work of the Holy Spirit. The potential of becoming like Jesus is miraculously present in us all. What is needed is for the believer to experience repeatedly the transforming work of the Holy Spirit which enables the surrendered person to reflect increasingly the glory of Jesus Christ in his or her life (2 Corinthians 3:17–18).

The Lord has provided a wonderful illustration of this very point through the miraculous life of my granddaughter, who is appropriately named Grace. On May 8, 2002 Grace Ryan Wardle came into the world thirteen weeks premature. She weighed only two pounds at delivery and was at high risk. The doctors and nurses immediately began to provide around-the-clock intensive care, doing everything possible to stabilize Grace and give her every possible chance at a full and healthy life.

There were many amazing facts about this journey to health for my precious granddaughter. One is relevant to this discussion and worth mentioning. Even at two pounds, Grace was born with every body part in place. Granted, her organs and limbs were weak and in some cases under-developed. Still, as tiny as Grace was, she had within her the potential for a healthy life. Grace was not missing something that would need to be provided at another time. All possibilities were already within her frail, little body. She simply needed time and attention to grow into her full potential as a human being.

Grace needs to receive proper nourishment to develop and sustain her physical health. She also needs nurture and love in order to grow emotionally in a safe and caring environment. She must be surrounded by people who will model psychological, spiritual, and emotional wellbeing. And in time Grace will need instruction and at times correction regarding all that life affords her in order to become mature and healthy. And as all this is provided and responded to correctly, Grace will mature into the person God designed her to be. And the growth that has already happened is wonderful to behold, for surely Grace is one of the Lord's precious gifts to the world.

What is true of the maturation process for Grace is an illustration of the path to growth for every person who responds to the call of Christ. In Peter's second epistle to the church he wrote, *"His divine power has given us everything we need for life and godliness"* (1:3). When a person accepts Christ a miraculous event happens. He is endowed by the Spirit with every potential for spiritual growth and maturity. The seed of Christ's nature is divinely implanted, holding the promise of Christ-likeness as he surrenders and co-operates with the transforming work of the Holy Spirit. The characteristics of Christ-likeness are already present, to be developed into maturity, that we may truly become like Jesus.

Nourish and Nurture

This process of transformation, which is an ongoing activity of the Holy Spirit, is not dissimilar to what I described in Grace's life. To mature in Christ a Christian needs ongoing nourishment. In this case, that involves feeding upon God's word, prayer, worship, and many other spiritual disciplines. These do not cause a person to be Christ-like, any more than food causes Grace to be human. Nourishment instead energizes the Christ-likeness that is already present, enabling it to grow and develop, again a work of the Holy Spirit.

The Christian also needs nurture to develop spiritual maturity. This is to come from the community of brothers and sisters who love as Christ loves, care as Christ cares, and protects as He protects. The level of affirmation and acceptance is critical to the process, and where withheld cripples believers significantly. Where love is generously given, growth happens in the best possible ways.

In addition, becoming like Jesus involves modeling by older, more mature believers. The day will come in Grace's life when her mom and dad will show her how to run, and jump, throw a ball, and shoot baskets. The potential is within herself, but modeling will help her develop more quickly. So it is with Christian maturity. The potential of Christ-likeness, present within the believer, will develop more quickly as mature believers model the characteristics and qualities of Jesus. For example, as mature believers walk secure in their identity, younger believers will better develop their own sense of being. And so it is with all the characteristics of Jesus discussed in this book. Modeling is part of the developmental process of becoming like Him.

And finally, there will need to be instruction and correction. When Grace learns to throw a ball, she will need to be taught that a window is not a good target for her to aim for when letting it fly. There are right ways and wrong ways to play ball. So it will be in the process of spiritual maturation. Once again consider the example of identity. A Christian has the potential within to be as confident as Christ that he or she is a child of God. That is good. However, the believer must never allow that to lead to a proud or discriminating heart. Instruction and correction under the guidance of the Holy Spirit are essential to the process of development. The church must provide such instruction, all the while knowing that the teaching does not contain the potential for Christ-likeness, only the ability to enhance its development in the surrendered and open believer. As nourishment, nurture, modeling, and instruction occur in the life of the believer maturation happens through the transforming activity of God's Spirit at work within.

I am convinced that this was what the Apostle Paul was writing about in Colossians. In verse 27 of chapter 1, Paul wrote that the glorious and mysterious richness of the gospel is, *"Christ in you."* He was saying that the seed of Christ's nature is present within every believer. Paul went on to say that he preached, admonished, and taught this to people so that they could become *"perfect in Christ,"* and that he was doing this work in the power of the Lord at work within him (Colossians 1:28–29). Paul then admonished his readers to live in Jesus continually, rooted, strengthened, and built up in Jesus, all with a thankful heart (Colossians 2:6–7).

Paul was describing the very issue being discussed in this chapter. Christians are to become like Jesus, perfected in Him by the power of the Holy Spirit. This maturation is not earned or won, it is developed from the seed of Christ already present in the believer's life. Preaching, teaching, admonishing, prayer, and many other channels of the Spirit's work are part of the developmental process. They are critical instruments of divine activity in a person's life. But the goal must always be clear and the heart surrendered to the process. Christians are to become like Jesus and so must daily position themselves for God's transforming work, offering every moment and event of life as part of the process. And as this happens, they will respond with a humble, yet incredibly thankful heart.

The Call of Christ

The call of Christ is an invitation for you to become like Him. No effort on your part could ever give you a chance of reaching that goal. But by His grace, and through the work of the Holy Spirit, the potential is there. What follows is a discussion of eight characteristics of the Christ-life that are at the very least in seed form within your life, a miraculous potential given by the Lord of love and grace. Each chapter will focus on one characteristic, how it was manifested in the life of Jesus, and what Scripture says about it regarding life as a follower of Jesus Christ. Each chapter will end with some suggestions regarding the nourishment and nurture process that is necessary to unleash these qualities. The implications of this for Christian maturity are tremendous. You will move far beyond the crisis of immaturity and begin to experience the radical nature of a transformed life.

Chapter 2

Identity

As a small boy I would get out of bed long before my parents so that I could be alone with my fantasies. While mom and dad slept I entered a magical world of make-believe. In those early morning hours I became someone special, a hero who was admired and respected by one and all. I would crawl across the hardwood floor pretending to be a soldier leading a group of troopers against a savage enemy hidden behind the living-room sofa, just like Rusty and Rin Tin Tin did every Saturday morning. At other times I became Roy Rogers, with pearl-handled six shooters at my sides, riding the arm of the couch as if it was Trigger, "the smartest horse in Hollywood." And then there were those wonderful mornings when I was Robin Hood, each piece of furniture a part of Sherwood Forest, the idyllic home of my own band of merry men. I dearly loved my world of make-believe, and was always sad when I had to hide it away within my heart whenever my family began to awaken to a new day.

Play and pretending are a normal part of a child's development. But there was more than psychological growth driving me to spend countless hours in a world of make-believe. I was wrestling with a deep desire to be someone special. For as long as I can remember, I struggled with an empty feeling inside, a painful longing to be a somebody.

That was not just true during my childhood, but throughout much of my life.

In junior high I was enthralled with the attention athletes received, especially the guys wearing letter sweaters. I wanted the respect and notoriety they were getting, so I set my course to be a letterman. I liked sports well enough, but it was not love of the game that drove me. I joined the team to get that coveted sweater. I even fantasized about wearing my letter sweater through the halls, watching others gaze at me with admiration and respect. But in the end the letter did not give me what I wanted. The sense of fulfillment lasted a mere moment, but the emptiness lingered on. So I had to look for other ways to become important.

In high school I added student government and drama to my plan for personal meaning. I thought maybe they would finally help me feel uniquely loved and accepted. But like everything else I tried, satisfaction was only momentary, while the ache inside grew more discomforting. On and on I went, trying to grab for my special seat at life's table. But I could not seem to find my place and so the hunger for significance continued to drive me.

Becoming a Christian should have settled the issue for me. But it didn't. I continued longing for worth and love, and tried to get some level of respect from my colleagues and the people I served. I practically worked myself to death, motivated by a strange mixture of love for Christ and a deep need to be seen by others as someone who counted. But no matter what I did, the ache continued, intensifying the older I became. I wanted to be a uniquely loved and gifted man, a person of special worth to others. But regardless of what I did, I still felt like an invisible man, incapable of being a special somebody to anybody.

This relentless struggle came to a head while I was teaching at an eastern seminary. I was in my mid-thirties and had a margin of success in my work. The board of trustees was looking for someone to lead the seminary to new growth. Somehow my name was submitted and after a thorough interview process I was invited to assume the position as the head of the institution. The personal affirmation that I received from the trustees through this offer was overwhelming. I could hardly believe that they saw me as a person who could assume such a great responsibility. While I was certainly fearful about the seriousness of the task, I was also elated. I had, in my view, finally become a somebody. After a brief time of prayer I took the job.

The moment I said yes an intense journey began that would ultimately lead to the discovery that being a somebody has nothing to do with power, or position, or pleasure. And anyone, who like me, attaches identity to such elusive and fickle entities is positioning himself for great heartache and trial. I embraced the job, not only as an opportunity to serve, but as an affirmation of personal meaning. That critical mistake ultimately contributed to a serious breakdown. I was capable of the task assigned to me by the trustees, but the responsibility did not fit my calling. Worse, it positioned me for serious conflict with people who disagreed with my vision for that institution. In a very short time what I thought to be the golden ring turned into handcuffs that enslaved me. The position did not help me rest secure in the special uniqueness that God had already provided for me. It only brought more disappointment and heartache.

Searching for Significance

I am not alone in the search for significance. People everywhere are wearing themselves out trying to find a way to stand out from the crowd and be recognized as a unique and special human being. We all share a common experience, a gnawing cry to be a somebody. There is nothing wrong with having such a need. It is a natural and God-given desire. What daily derails us is the way we try to fulfill that longing. We strive to gain a sense of individual worth through money, power, popularity, appearance, relationships, position, ability, and performance. We seem to believe that if we can just be richer, stronger, prettier, or more popular than others we will finally stand out from the crowd and satisfy the inner hunger for importance. But it is all a lie sending us on an endless search for a place to stand in a land of perpetual quicksand.

There are two dominant characteristics of people who seek to find their uniqueness through the items listed previously: anxiety and competition. People live with a chronic, though at times subconscious, sense of restlessness. This matter of identity is very important to a person's sense of wellbeing. No one wants to feel like he or she is simply an unidentifiable face in a crowd. Everyone wants to know that they matter and have that special place at the table of life. However, a person should never link his or her identity to anything that can be lost. To attach identity to such elusive entities means that there is always the ever-looming threat that the uniqueness being experienced is only temporary, subject to change at any moment. And there is no doubt that all of the items listed earlier can be lost in a heartbeat.

Athletic ability wanes, appearance changes with age, financial security can be disrupted, jobs can be taken away, and relationships do not last forever. Those who invest in such things as the answer to identity-needs, repeatedly find that the pursuit never ends. Anxiety becomes a constant companion. It is easy to see that this is true. Consider how many people worry about money, appearance, position, power, and popularity. They are part of the daily conversation of life and receive heavy investments from desperate people. Why? Because to countless men and women these things mean the difference between personal importance and endless insignificance. That is a tremendous weight to place upon items that do not ultimately deliver what they promise. Deep inside people know this, but do not seem able to stop the insanity. The deep ache is simply too great, and so the striving continues, even when the satisfaction is fleeting at best.

Competition is also a by-product of searching for love in the wrong places. Inherent in the desperate quest for identity through power, position, and popularity is the need to be better than others. Buying into this system means that a person must be richer than, better than, stronger than, more powerful than someone else in order to feel special. This attitude is at the core of the very worst in bigotry, discrimination, and social injustice. Being special and a winner necessitates that there be someone who is designated as less special and a loser. The only way for a person in this system to advance is at the expense of someone else. The joy and celebration of the person who finally achieved his or her goal can only take place when someone else is crying because he or she did not make the cut.

How well I remember the day I made the local little league team. It was a tremendous feeling to be chosen, a first step I thought to being important. As I walked toward the car overwhelmed with joy I noticed my friend Dennis crying. I realized that he had not been selected. It was no less important to him than it was to me, for we were both desperate to make the cut. We both wanted to be part of the chosen few. But there were only sixteen uniforms, and I received the last one. For me to make the team, Dennis had to be passed over. Granted, much of life is like that. But what compounds the problem is this issue of identity. It is tough enough to be passed over in life, but when significance is attached to the matter, it can be devastating.

Dennis and I were caught in a terrible place. He could not rejoice with me, and I could not afford to alleviate his suffering by giving up my place on the team. Our identities were at risk, and as much as our friendship meant to each other, the desperate need to be special was superimposed upon the relationship. Competition was the name of the game. And we were only eight-year-old boys who could barely throw a baseball! Life only gets more complicated the older and more invested we become. When personal identity is not securely grounded it makes it very difficult to give away power, position, and popularity in order to serve another. Selfishness prevails, which leads to ungodly pride for the chosen and debilitating shame for those who must live watching life from the cheap seats.

Is this what Jesus intended for His followers? Did He mean for believers to live in chronic anxiety, striving to find significance through power, position, and popularity, all the while knowing that it could be swept away in a moment? Can competition be the way of Christ, where people find meaning by ascending on the backs of those who do not gain the prize? If one were to answer those questions based upon what is happening in the lives of Christians, each would be answered yes.

The Church is full of people anxiously striving to ascend in life at the expense of others. Many of these people are leaders, including some who preach every Sunday. That is part of the crisis of immaturity. People may be clear about what to believe, but they live in constant insecurity because their identities are at risk. But none of this is the way of Jesus. He was absolutely secure in His identity and invites Christians everywhere to become like Him through the

transforming power of the Holy Spirit. There is a place of
security and rest from all this striving, and it is found in the
seed of Christ present within every believer.

Jesus Is the Beloved Son of God

There are many things about the life and ministry of Jesus
that are amazing and wonderful. But two specific insights
from the Gospels are directly relevant to the topic of personal
identity. First, Jesus was unwilling to compromise His calling
from God, no matter how good the alternative appeared to
be. Second, He was able to descend to where people were
caught in the very depths of human depravity in order to
serve and rescue the broken. He did this willingly, fully
engaged emotionally and overflowing with love for lost
people. These two abilities give clear evidence that Jesus knew
who He was and was secure in His place at the table of God.

The Gospel of John contains the familiar story of the
feeding of five thousand people with fives loaves and two
small fishes. Virtually every Christian, and countless non-
Christians, are familiar with that wonderful miracle, where
Jesus brings abundance out of so little when it is offered with
a pure heart. But John does not end the story until he
records the reaction of the crowd to what Jesus did. They
were so taken by the event that they wanted Jesus to become
king and they were prepared to make Him say yes, even if it
took force. They were convinced that He was the prophet
promised to come and deliver them from bondage (John
6:14–15).

What an appealing offer! Jesus could have moved toward
Jerusalem with a great crowd of insurrectionists, assumed
leadership of the nation and led people to a freedom they
had not known for years. The people were enthralled with
His ability and dedicated to serve Him. They were probably

in an emotional frenzy, excited to make Jesus king. Talk about personal affirmation! But He would have none of it. The will of the people and adulation of the crowd would not cause Jesus to sway from His God-appointed calling. John records that Jesus simply left the excited people and withdrew to a mountain hideaway where He could be alone (John 6:15). Unlike me, Jesus did not say yes to an opportunity because it would somehow make Him feel like a somebody. He was secure in His identity and unwavering in His determination to stay faithful to the Father's will.

Jesus Was Secure Enough to Serve

Jesus also was secure enough in His identity to serve others, even when they were at the very bottom of life. Jesus was the Suffering Servant of Isaiah 53. He completely emptied Himself of all position and glory in order to care for the broken. And doing this cost Him greatly. Jesus suffered in order to serve, even to the point of giving His life so that others could escape the cold darkness of eternal death. Jesus walked with the impoverished, ate with the sinner, touched the leprous, embraced the rejected, and loved the unlovable. He gave where others would have taken, set free when the less secure would have enslaved, and lifted up those whom others tried to put down. There was no competition in His heart or even a hint of desire to advance on the back of another person. Jesus, secure in His identity, was the prince who became a pauper so that every pauper could become a prince.

On the night Jesus was to be betrayed He gathered with His disciples for a last supper. John records the event in his Gospel and begins the narrative with an amazing description of the ministry of Jesus to those He loved. John wrote that Jesus wanted to show His disciples the full extent of His love, so He took off His outer clothing, wrapped a towel around His waist, and washed the disciples' feet (John 13:3–14). This act of self-emptying was so shocking that the disciples did not know how to respond. He should have been the honored guest. They should have washed His feet, humbled themselves before Him. Instead, it was Jesus who willingly took up the tools of a servant, towel and basin, to bless those that He loved. Jesus knelt before them all, even the one who was already positioned to betray Him. This act was a metaphor for the entire life of Jesus, and clear evidence that Jesus knew who He was and rested secure in His identity.

Jesus did not define Himself by position, power, or popularity. Instead He knew that God was His Father and He the Beloved Son. That was the rooting of His personal identity, a relationship of love that He knew He could never lose. Jesus was not seduced to search for significance through the adoration of the crowd, the promise of wealth or fame, or the prospect of being elevated to a position of political leadership. None of that was alluring because He already was at peace that He was a somebody. He did not wrestle with identity anxiety, nor did He compete with people for place and meaning. He had all that and more through His standing as God's Son.

Secure in the Father's Love

The Gospels reveal that God wanted Jesus to be confident of the fact that He was His Beloved Son. Matthew, Mark, and Luke each include the two separate occasions when the Father spoke and the heavens opened above Jesus. The first event occurs at the baptism of Christ in the Jordan river. As Jesus comes up out of the water the Spirit descends upon Him as a dove and God speaks these words:

"You are my Son, whom I love; with you I am well pleased."
(Mark 1:11)

God knew what Jesus was going to face as He stepped into public ministry. There would be temptation, trial, unbelievable human demand, countless opportunities to be seduced from His mission, denial and betrayal from close friends, and ultimately death on the cross. It was as if God were saying, "No matter what anyone says or does, be secure in this, you are my Son and I love you." God restated this truth three years later during the Transfiguration, telling all who were there that He loved Jesus, once again declaring that Jesus was God's Son (Mark 9:7). God wanted no question in Christ's heart: He was calling Jesus to root Himself in His position with the Father. This identity confidence was part of what enabled Jesus to stay the path, even when it led to Calvary. Jesus knew He had a secure place in life, and that He was special in a way that could never be lost or compromised. What gave Jesus meaning? The fact that He was God's Son and dearly loved by Him.

Did Jesus believe what the Father said? The Gospels once again provide the answer. When people asked Jesus why He did the things He did, He pointed to the Father and His love. Jesus said,

> *"I tell you the truth, the Son can do nothing by himself; he can only do what he sees his Father doing, because whatever the Father does the Son also does. For the Father loves the Son and shows him all he does."* (John 5:19–20)

When the Pharisees questioned Jesus about His claims to be the light of the world, He again pointed to His relationship with the Father. He told them that what He said was true and that His Father, who sent Him, was the witness to His claim (John 8:12–18). Later, when they questioned what Jesus was saying about the Father, He told them that He only spoke what He heard the Father say and that the Father was always with Him. He then concluded by affirming that the Father was with Him and never left Him alone. Jesus ended His response by declaring that He always did what pleased the Father (John 8:27–29).

Jesus based the definition of His life upon His relationship with God. He knew that God was His Father and He the beloved Son. This identity confidence served as the anchor to His entire life and ministry. There was no seeking the approval of others to try to gain worth, no fighting for recognition, grabbing for power, or desperation for fame. He did not try to please people to get a measure of love; He did not worry about financial security, or strive to be better than anyone else. Jesus knew who He was and that security served as the foundation of His life. Jesus, the Beloved of God, needed nothing more to identify Him as special. He walked this earth confident that He was the Father's Son.

We Are the Father's Beloved Children

The Good News of the gospel of Christ begins with this amazing fact. We Christians, new creations through the transforming work of the Holy Spirit, have received the seed of Christ's nature. This wonderful reality holds many promises, not the least of which is the amazing gift of being the children of God. What was true of Jesus as He lived on earth is equally true of all who embrace Christ as Redeemer and Lord. We, like Jesus, are the Beloved of God. Our identities are securely rooted in our relationship with the Heavenly Father as His special and dearly loved children.

There is no reason for Christians to struggle constantly in order to gain a sense of uniqueness. We do not need to live with that gnawing undercurrent of anxiety, nor relentlessly compete with others to be special. God, through Christ, has given us what we could never earn, win, or achieve. He has transformed us into His children, and placed at our disposal all the resources of the Kingdom as fully adopted heirs. And, through His promises, we can rest secure that this uniqueness can never be stolen or taken away. There is no need to worry, strive, or fight to protect. We no longer need to have more than others, be better than others, or feel more important than others to be a somebody. We hold the seed of Christ-likeness in the deepest part of our inner being.

When Paul wrote to the Christians in Ephesus, he told them that they were dearly loved children of God (Ephesians 5:1). He wanted them to know that Christ had radically transformed them and they should now seek to grow and develop according to their standing as children of light. Paul did not want them to continue in the destructive beliefs and lifestyle of unbelievers. He saw these as unhealthy and unnecessary. The riches of Christ were now at their disposal and they could walk with confidence in their position as God's children.

How sad it is to see Christians continue to this day struggling with identity issues. They grab for meaning and uniqueness from the most illusive and unsatisfying things, all the while having standing in the universe as the beloved of God. This is a strategy of the evil one aimed at keeping Christians from the confidence and freedom that is theirs in Christ Jesus. This identity crisis is crippling countless believers and hindering the ministry of the Church.

Paul recognized that the Ephesians, like many Christians, needed to mature into the fullness of who they were in Jesus. He did not want them to languish in immaturity, but instead desired that they grow to be like Jesus, which is the true goal of the faith. To do this they had to understand their potential as the children of God and discover the unsearchable riches of Christ that indwelled them. Paul listed many of these blessings within his letter to the church of Ephesus. The list includes:

- blessed in the heavenly realms (Ephesians 1:3)
- chosen (Ephesians 1:4)
- holy (Ephesians 1:4)
- blameless (Ephesians 1:4)
- redeemed (Ephesians 1:7)
- forgiven (Ephesians 1:7)
- lavished upon (Ephesians 1:8)
- in Christ (Ephesians 1:13)
- marked with the Spirit (Ephesians 1:13)
- made alive with Christ (Ephesians 2:5)
- seated with Christ in heaven (Ephesians 2:6)
- God's work of art (Ephesians 2:10)
- brought near to God (Ephesians 2:13)
- a dwelling for the Holy Spirit (Ephesians 2:22)
- rooted in love (Ephesians 3:17)
- gifted (Ephesians 4:11)
- filled with the Spirit (Ephesians 5:18)
- strong in the Lord (Ephesians 6:10)
- armed for battle (Ephesians 6:13–17)

This is but a partial list of the unsearchable riches of Christ implanted within every believer. The nature of Christ that indwells Christians is beyond measure, providing a uniqueness that is unequalled in the entire universe. We Christians are special beyond words, important to the God of all creation. We enjoy a position even angels cannot experience, given by Christ as an incomparable gift of grace. How insignificant money is in light of the inheritance we hold in Jesus. Why seek fame as a way to be special when all heaven already knows your name? What position could ever compare to prince and princess of the Lord Most High? Who needs to climb over the backs of others to find meaning when they are already seated beside Christ in the throne room of God? When would Christians ever find the need for worldly power when they have within them the power that raised Jesus from the dead?

The very last thing Christians should struggle with is an identity crisis. We are His beloved children. In light of what is true of us in Christ, the very thought seems silly, even childish. Which is precisely the point of this entire discussion. Countless Christians are caught in a crisis of immaturity, battling a deep sense of identity anxiety and confusion? Why? Because leaders have failed to nourish and nurture the seed of Christ's identity that indwells believers, enabling them to grow mature in the likeness of Christ. They may teach the essential doctrines of the faith, but the seed of Christ's nature goes undeveloped. Yet the Holy Spirit of the Lord is ready and willing to work in every receptive heart, moving the surrendered Christian into increasing security in their identity in Christ.

Nourishment and Nurture

The first step toward maturity in this matter is recognition and repentance. You must realize the futility of linking your identity to power, position, and popularity. More specifically, I encourage you to identify prayerfully the unhealthy places where you turn to gain importance. You should allow the Lord to show you where you invest in a futile effort to be a somebody. Once identified, it would be helpful if you consider all the time, energy, worry, and loss that has been wrapped up in that endless pursuit. It would not take long before you realize that there has been far more heartache than help from all this striving.

Repentance always involves a turning. In this case it would involve looking away from the way of the world and facing Christ. He has provided more than you could ever ask or think, gracing you with standing and position before the Father. You would do well to confess the error, or more directly stated sin, of trying to find personal meaning in power, position, and popularity; and, through the in-dwelling Spirit, you should seek to grow into a mature believer who stands humbly confident of all that is yours in Christ.

Nourishment and nurture also involve turning to God's word in order to discover all that is true of you regarding your identity. The list from Ephesians is a great place to start. I have found it immensely helpful to seek the Spirit's help in understanding and maturing in the riches of my inheritance in Christ Jesus. I regularly meditate upon one of the truths Paul lists in Ephesians regarding my identity, asking that the Holy Spirit take its reality deep within my soul. By His power an ongoing transformation occurs which enables me to say no to the world's answer to my identity needs, and rest ever more securely in who I am in Christ. Granted, this growth is not instantaneous and there is temptation once again to question my place, though God has already declared it secure in Him. However, as I continue to soak in the word that God has stated, that I am His beloved child, the power of the world diminishes, and the freedom of my new identity increases.

It is no less important that you gather together with other Christians to reaffirm the truth of your being God's dearly loved children. The church should be a gathering of the beloved, where words are spoken and lessons taught that encourage people to rest in the promises of God. Jesus has made people new and endowed them with riches and wonders beyond description. That message should be shouted from the pulpits with hearts bursting with praise. That will do far more to establish people mature in Christ than much of the negativism that can be found in most churches. There is good news. You have, by grace, become the child of God. That is your eternal identity.

You are to become increasingly like Jesus. That alone is the goal of Christian life and the true sign of maturity. Thankfully, the seed of that maturity has already been planted deep within you, and the Holy Spirit is constant to nourish and nurture that inner life into spiritual adulthood, if you surrender to His work. The people of Christ are to be a transformed people, and the foundation of that radical work rests in the reality that we belong to God. There is no longer a need to strive, grab, please people, or compete in order to find a place at the table. Our identity as God's beloved is all we will ever need.

Chapter 3

Intimacy

Intimate love defies description. At least that is true for me. The experience of true love is so powerful and transforming that it is in many ways beyond words. Even if I were the most gifted writer or artist the world has ever known, the image would still fall far short of the reality, the description would be a mere shadow of the real thing. I just cannot adequately describe all the feelings that simultaneously converge within me when love begins to flow from heart to heart.

No matter what I might say about resting in the arms of my wife, or cherishing the presence of my children, or holding my granddaughter close to my breast, or experiencing the contentment that comes when I am with my friends, it would only provide a glimpse into the experience. The depth of feeling is so great that it is essentially unfathomable. At best, I can describe some of the ingredients of this love, knowing that what I write would only enable a person to look merely into the window of my heart. I know that for me love involves a *desire* that is almost consuming. No matter how much I am with those I love, there is always a hunger for more. Love also brings *contentment and confidence*. I find that when I leave those I love I am content as I carry them in my heart, and confident that love

39

will still be there when I return. And there is *delight* in love, a feeling of unequaled pleasure in the presence of those I cherish. It is not what they do that excites me, it is just the fact that they are there, alive and real.

I also know that love involves *vulnerability*, a seeing and being seen that is honest and in more ways than one, uncovered. For that to be true, love demands a *risk* and *acceptance*. True love involves seeing one another as we really are, strengths and weakness, beauty and imperfection combined. That involves taking the risk to be real, and then discovering that I am received, just as I am. When love is present I also feel *protected* and *protective*. I sense that I am safe in love's embrace and at the same time watchful that nothing harms those who have a place within my heart. And then there is *passion* in love, which I can only describe as a relentless longing to be forever connected to those I love, finding its ultimate expression in the exclusive experience of sensual embrace with my wife. Beyond all this, I can only say that love is a glorious mystery of life.

The greatest discovery of my life came when the Lord revealed to me that He feels all of this for me. I was aware that the Scripture speaks repeatedly about God being love and Jesus giving His life for us because of love. But somehow I never really considered that this truth was intended to translate into an actual experience of His love. I somehow limited the relational component of my faith to categories of respect, honor, loyalty, servanthood, and obedience. Oh, I am sure that I knew that God would protect me with His love and provide for my most important needs. But it did not even cross my mind to consider that the Lord would have desire for me, experience delight in my presence, or somehow feel passionate toward me. Such notions were simply unthinkable. He was God and I a sinner, so how could such feelings have anything to do with the way He would relate to me?

This immature concept of what it meant to be in relationship to God significantly limited my Christian walk. While I sought to give all I had in service to the Lord, there was a nagging emptiness deep inside, a void that could not be satisfied through the love of friends and family. Something was not right and I continually struggled with an indefinable loneliness. Respect, honor, loyalty, servanthood, and obedience were increasingly not enough. A painful awakening began to take place in my soul, initiated by the Holy Spirit, which gave me the desperation and courage to cry out to God for more. This began a journey that has literally transformed my life and ministry. I have, by His good grace, discovered that God is passionate, full of love and desire for His children. And Jesus Christ delights in His followers and longs to ravish His bride, the Church. This love is real, can be experienced in this life, and is available to all who have said yes to His call.

What type of relationship do you have with Christ? If you are like most Christians, you are respectful of Christ, and seek to honor Him with your service. You are probably faithful and loyal, and careful to behave according to Christian standards, even to the point of living sacrificial lifestyles. But are you regularly having times of intimate embrace with Christ? Is your relationship deepening and developing spiritual maturity in your life?

Obstacles to Intimacy

If the truth be told, many Christians feel that something is missing in their relationship with the Lord, yet they seem unclear as to the source of the problem or its solution. Be assured that the problem is not with Jesus. He is more than willing to engage in intimate embrace with His followers. Jesus is the Lord of love and has already proven the extent to which He will go to be united with believers. He wants to lavish love upon us and is already positioned to engage in a relationship that is unequalled in depth and intensity.

If then, we are desperate to be loved, and Jesus is passionate about giving love, why do so many Christians suffer from relational immaturity? Why would there be such an undercurrent of frustration, dissatisfaction, and loneliness within the Christian community? I would suggest that there are five primary reasons, any one of which could significantly hinder a person's experience of intimacy with the Lord:

1. Prioritizing right thinking over right relationship
2. An unhelpful metaphor of the Christian life
3. Being unaware of the invitation to intimacy
4. Fear of vulnerability
5. Not knowing how to position for Christ's loving embrace

Each of these issues could be the focus of lengthy discussion. I intend to address each briefly, and then move into a more detailed treatment of intimacy in the life of Jesus and His invitation for you to engage in intimate embrace with Him.

The first obstacle that many people face regarding relational intimacy with Christ is the unhealthy prioritizing of right thinking over right relationship. I mentioned this matter in chapter 1, and will again highlight the issue here. There has been an unfortunate emphasis upon knowing propositional truth about the Christian faith as the key to the Christian life. Many pastors and Christian leaders are intent on making sure that the people they serve believe the right things. I agree that this has importance. But the teachings of Scripture need to be understood and embraced, not because Christians are going to face some test, but so that it enhances their relationship with the Lord. Beliefs and doctrines of the faith must be more than propositional facts. They should be truths for life. The goal of our faith is a dynamic relationship with Jesus, not the accumulation of facts and beliefs. Christianity is about a living relationship with Jesus and truth should be taught in ways that deepen that reality in the life of believers.

Second, more than a few Christians struggle with the concept of intimacy with the Lord because of a metaphor often used to describe the Christian life. I have more than once heard preachers tell people that salvation can be likened to a trial. We, the sinner are standing before the judge, God, guilty of disobeying the law and deserving of death. But, as sentence is about to be pronounced, Jesus steps forward on our behalf. He tells the judge that we belong to Him and declares that He will pay the full penalty for our offense. The judge accepts this offer and sets us forever free from the death we had deserved, giving us eternal life in Christ Jesus.

There is a problem with the metaphor. It is based upon a legal paradigm, which falls terribly short of the relational nature of the Christian experience. The notion of being freed by a judge does not endear people to develop a relationship with the judge. Friendship, let alone intimacy, is seldom considered part of the equation. If I were actually released from punishment for some crime, I would not want to go back to the judge's chamber for a visit. I would stay away, not wanting to run the risk of him changing his mind.

A far more accurate metaphor for the Christian faith is the incarnation. Jesus, moved by passionate love, does everything possible to be united with those who call out to Him in faith. He enters our world in order to lead people into levels of increasing intimacy with Him. That journey begins with the cleansing work of repentance and continues throughout life until Christians enter His heavenly bridal chamber. Using the incarnation as the primary metaphor of faith helps people understand and embrace the deeply relational nature of following Jesus Christ.

Third, there are Christians who do not know that Jesus desires an intimate relationship with them. I was riding through Northern California with a well-known Christian speaker. In the course of our conversation I mentioned that my heart was aching for a deeper intimacy with the Lord. He looked rather stunned, and after a few moments said, "I see myself as a man under orders. I receive my instructions from God and then set out to do what He commands. I have not even considered that intimacy with Christ is even available or necessary." That may sound servant-like and obedient, but there is something deeply wrong with that concept of Christian living.

Jesus told His followers that they were far more than servants. They were His friends (John 15:13–15). Jesus went to incredible lengths to be close to His followers, spending great amounts of time being involved in their lives and making space for them in His life. He once said that knowing Him and the Father is the key to eternal life (John 17:3). The "knowing" was intimate and experiential, not academic and propositional. More time will be given to this aspect of the life of Jesus later in the chapter. It is enough to say here that the invitation to intimacy is for every person who responds to the call of Christ.

Fourth, there are people who fear intimacy with the Lord. At one level I totally understand that. After all Jesus is the Son of the Living God. The thought of coming into His presence can be frightening, compounded when it involves drawing into His loving embrace. His power can be intimidating. And His purity and holiness can be absolutely unnerving. More than a few people have told me that they feel unworthy to ask the Lord for that level of relationship. They fear that He will see all their impurities and inadequacies, and either scold them or reject them outright. However, that is not how Jesus sees His followers.

As stated in the previous chapter, Jesus relates to Christians according to their new nature that has been implanted within them by God's grace. Jesus looks at believers as children of God, full of incredible wonder and potential as new creations. Granted, Christians need to grow. But Jesus knows that and invites believers to draw near with confidence, experiencing the transforming power of His intimate presence. The more time Christians spend with the Lord, the more they begin to look like Him, the true sign of spiritual growth and maturity.

Finally, many Christians do not know how to develop relational intimacy with the Lord. Even if they are aware of the invitation to enter the Lord's embrace, they do not seem to be able to find the pathway to His presence. Many try to get there through performance-based discipleship models, but grow frustrated when such efforts do not actually help them meet the Lord in increasing levels of intimacy. Some then conclude that this level of relationship is not really available to them, and sadly give up on the entire idea.

A Pathway toward Intimacy

There is a pathway to the Lord's embrace that can be found by everyone who names Jesus Christ as Lord. Experiencing God is not limited to spiritual superstars, but is instead a possibility for every child of God. Like all relationships this intimacy takes time and involves deepening levels of trust and vulnerability. At the end of this chapter, in the section on nourishing and nurturing the seed of Christ's nature within every believer, I will discuss five principles that help Christians position themselves for relational intimacy. It is enough here simply to mention these ideas and restate that the pathway to God's presence is open to all believers, everywhere.

- It is the Holy Spirit who brings people into the Presence of God.
- Sacred space enhances relational intimacy.
- Christians must give time to God if they want to develop relational intimacy.
- Believers need to become attentive to God's presence within every moment of every day.
- Spiritual disciplines enable Christians to catch the wind of the Spirit and move toward the embrace of God.

God did not intend for His children to have a passionless relationship with Him. Respect, honor, loyalty, and obedience are important. But God is a loving Father who desires to lavish love upon His own. He wants to move Christians beyond relational immaturity, into a level of intimacy that is literally transforming. He wants to replace emptiness with the fullness of His love, sadness with deep joy, and loneliness with the abiding confidence that He is ever present with those He loves. Nowhere is this more clearly communicated than through the life and ministry of Jesus Christ.

Jesus and the Call to Relational Maturity

Once again we consider the call to become like Jesus. We have already established the fact that the seed of Christ's nature has been supernaturally implanted within every person who has been born of the Spirit. That means that we have the potential to become more and more like Jesus. The journey toward Christ-likeness involves the constant ministry of the Holy Spirit and takes ongoing nourishment and nurture. But the characteristics of Christ can be developed in the lives of His followers, moving us increasingly forward toward spiritual maturity.

We are looking at the call to intimacy with God. There are three truths that we can learn about God's desire to be in relationship with us from the life and teachings of Jesus. First, Jesus went out of His way to be close to His followers. Second, He had a deep and intimate relationship with His heavenly Father. And third, Jesus made it possible for Christians to have that same type of intimate relationship with God and with Him.

First, I am continually amazed at the lengths to which Jesus went to reconcile people with God. Rather than stay in heaven in all His divine glory, Jesus emptied Himself and became human in order to save all humankind. John wrote that Jesus, the very expression of God, became flesh and made His dwelling with people (John 1:14). Paul spoke of this in Philippians when he wrote that Jesus *"made himself nothing, taking the very nature of a servant, being made in human likeness"* (Philippians 2:7). Jesus, the Eternal Son of God, came as a baby, was born and raised in poverty, lived in relative obscurity, and faced incredible opposition, all to draw people close to Himself and the Father. The world has never before or since seen such an example of *agape* love. And Jesus did this because He desired intimacy with ordinary people, just like you and me. All we need do is respond to His invitation.

I was impacted by the story that is found in John 1:24–42. John the Baptist is standing near the Jordan with two of his disciples. Jesus passes by and John declares, *"Look, the Lamb of God."* The two disciples begin to follow Jesus. Christ turns at one point and asks what they want. They say they want to know where Jesus is staying, to which the Lord responds, *"Come and see"* (NKJV). The Gospel says that they go with Jesus and stay with Him throughout the entire day.

As I meditated upon this narrative I was deeply moved by how accessible Jesus was to these two men. He opened up His life to them. Jesus, the Son of God, the Eternal Word, Lord of all creation, welcomed them into His intimate space. One can see this repeatedly through the Gospels, as Jesus eats with people, shares His life with them, teaches them Kingdom truths, walks with them, and embraces them into His heart. Jesus opened His life to His followers in the most tender and intimate way. His arms were extended wide, inviting people to experience the depth of His matchless love. And what Jesus did then with the disciples He does now with all Christians. He is not standing at a distance holding people at arm's length. Jesus has proven that He will even pay the ultimate price of His life to be deeply united to those He loves. He invites us into His life and in turn desires that we completely open our lives to Him. We need to draw near to Him with great faith, trusting His invitation to intimate fellowship.

Second, Jesus' life on earth was marked by an intimate relationship with the heavenly Father. I previously discussed the two times when the Father spoke from heaven and declared that Jesus was His Son. These encounters with God not only related to the identity of Jesus, but also pointed to the intimate relationship the Father had with the Son. In both cases the Father spoke of His love for Jesus. This love was foundational to the Lord's life and ministry.

Jesus also spoke openly of His loving relationship with the Father. He repeatedly said that He was in the Father and the Father was in Him (John 10:38; 14:11; 17:21). Jesus shared deep intimacy with God the Father. Read the Gospels and you see that He was passionate about His love for God. There was intense desire and delight in Jesus' relationship. He was connected to the Father in every way possible. Jesus loved the Father, regularly spent time in His presence, and was dependent upon Him for strength, guidance, and help. He not only obeyed Him, Jesus worshiped the Father and openly expressed His devotion to Him. Throughout His ministry Jesus would get away from the crowd to spend time before the Father in prayer. He prayed when He wanted the Father's guidance (Mark 1:35), when He chose the disciples (Luke 6:12), when He interceded for His followers (John 17), and when He was agonizing in Gethsemane (Matthew 26:39). Finally, He cried out to the Father from the cross (Matthew 27:46). Jesus was deeply connected to the Father and His love.

Jesus lived His entire life in intimate union with God. He repeatedly made reference to the fact that this union determined what He said and did. Jesus told the disciples that everything He had belonged to the Father, and everything the Father had was His (John 17:10). The relationship Jesus had with the heavenly Father was marked by something greater than honor, respect, loyalty, and obedience. Theirs was a relationship of the most intimate love. This love had depth of feeling and devotion.

Third, Jesus clearly invited His followers to have the same intimate relationship with the Father that He had. That may sound too good to be true, but Scripture is very clear on this point. When Jesus was interceding for His followers during Passion Week He made an amazing statement. He said,

"I have made you known to them, and will continue to make you known in order that the love you have for me may be in them and that I myself may be in them." (John 17:26)

The phrase *"that the love you have for me may be in them"* is very important to this discussion. Jesus intended to make a way for all His followers to experience God's intimate love in their lives. He wanted them to experience the desire, delight, and passion from God that He did. He even told His disciples that He and the Father wanted to come and make their home with all those who loved and obeyed Jesus (John 14:23).

What an incredible invitation! The Father and Son, through the ministry of the Holy Spirit, invite Christians to step into the Father's arms of love. Jesus had that level of intimacy with the Father, and now welcomes His followers into that same transforming embrace. Christianity is all about love that is wide, and deep, and beyond understanding. This experience of intimacy is not reserved for a select group of super-saints. It is for all who name Christ as Lord. Jesus came all the way from heaven to earth to share this good news, and gave His life to provide a way for us all.

We have already established the fact that Christians are to become like Jesus. A central characteristic of Christ's life was His intimate, passionate, exciting relationship with the Father. The seed of His nature now indwells His followers, which means that we too can grow to experience the intimacy that Jesus shared. Some may wonder if it is really possible. It is more than possible. It is essential to spiritual maturity. Anything less is but a shadow of the true relationship that God intends for His children. We were created for intimacy with God and are ultimately headed for eternity in His embrace. The seed of Christ's relationship to the Father is within us. It is now a matter of allowing the Holy Spirit to nourish and nurture that potential into an experienced and transforming reality.

Nourishment and Nurture

I am convinced that every Christian has a longing to have a regular experience of the Lord's presence. That ache is evidence that people were made to commune with the Lord and only God's love can fill that deep need.

Only Jesus can satisfy the cry of the human heart and He opens His arms to receive the willing into His intimate embrace. The question of course is, "How does that happen?"

The most helpful description of the journey to the Lord's embrace comes from the illustration of sailing. I once had the opportunity to chase gray whales off the coast of Mexico. The entire experience was exhilarating to me. I felt like all my senses were alive as we raced across the water under the power of the wind. Doing that involved a certain amount of skill and attention from the captain. He sat at the helm guiding the rudder toward the desired destination. He had to watch for other vessels, all the while looking for the whales and maneuvering close enough to see them on their yearly journey south. The captain also had to set the sails properly and attend to rigging in order to catch the wind so that we could move along on the journey.

Experiencing intimacy with the Lord is much like that. To journey toward Christ you must understand the basic principles of devotional intimacy. And the first and most important principle is that "wind" is an absolute necessity. Again, consider what we can learn from sailing. While the helm and rudder and sails and rigging are necessary, without wind they are all useless. They have no power in themselves to move the vessel along its plotted course. The captain could wear himself out adjusting the sails, positioning the rudder, setting the rigging, trying to move the ship along. He could even command the entire crew to blow into the sails. But all that activity would amount to nothing. It is all a matter of wind.

So it is with the journey to God's embrace. There are activities that you can do to catch the wind of the Spirit. I will briefly highlight four. But these efforts are, in themselves, powerless. They cannot advance you a single foot toward the Lord's embrace. Movement and the experience of intimacy demand the activity of the Holy Spirit. All performance-oriented attempts to cause growth and develop spiritual maturity will end in exhaustion and frustration. The journey to intimacy with God demands the Breath of God. That means that you must seek the Holy Spirit's help on this journey to intimacy, surrendering to His presence and power. You need to tell the Spirit about your heart's desire and submit to His leading.

First, just as the captain of a sailing vessel must take the helm, so you must develop sacred space in your life. John the Baptist had the wilderness, Jesus the Mount of Olives, and countless Christians through the ages have had special places where they met alone with the Lord. If you desire intimacy with God you should consider designating a special place as your special "chamber" for meeting Jesus. Granted, you can grow to where all of life is sacred space. But a first step toward that is to create an actual place for devotional intimacy. This sacred space should be quiet, comfortable, and conducive to uninterrupted fellowship with the Lord. Symbols and music could enhance the atmosphere, each preparing the person to experience the Holy Spirit's presence and power.

Time is a second prerequisite to catching the wind of the Spirit. The wise captain knows that there will be calm seas, with little wind to power the vessel. At those times he waits faithfully. So it is with devotional intimacy. You must learn to give time for experiencing the embrace of God. Spiritual maturity does not happen to people who live life at a hectic pace. Just as building relationships with people takes time, so does developing intimacy with God. You should set aside enough time, daily, weekly, even yearly, to experience the presence of the Lord through the empowerment of the Holy Spirit. There is no way to predict how much time that means. That depends upon the "Wind." The key to the journey toward intimacy with God is to actually go to that sacred space regularly and anticipate the Breath of God.

Third, the journey toward God's embrace demands becoming attentive to His presence in all of life. Every minute of every day is full of the Lord's presence. Unfortunately most believers are unaware of the wonder of each divine moment and go about life blind to His activity. They are unable to recognize where the Lord is moving and discern what He is doing. You need to ask the Holy Spirit to give you eyes to see and ears to hear. He will help you find God in each moment and learn to respond appropriately. This gift of attentiveness will help you position yourself for divine embrace and then rest there in the transforming love of the Lord.

Finally, as the captain needs sails to catch the wind, you need spiritual disciplines. Throughout church history believers have practiced a wide variety of spiritual exercises that positioned them to meet the Lord. In themselves the disciplines are powerless to move people into the presence of the Lord. But these disciplines have been known to be wonderful sails for catching the wind of the Holy Spirit. And I have learned that the more sails one sets, the more he or she has opportunity to move forward toward the Lord's embrace. What follows is a brief list of several disciplines that can serve you on this journey.

- *Solitude:* Choosing to come apart from daily activity in order to be alone with God.

- *Silence:* Choosing against the noise of the world in order to listen to the whispers of God.

- *Fasting:* Abstaining from food for a specific period of time in order to lessen the grip the flesh has upon lives and open the way to experiencing God's strength in weakness.

- *Secrecy:* Consciously choosing to follow the admonition of Jesus and do deeds of service and giving in private.

- *Sacrifice:* Giving beyond ability in response to God's self-giving.

- *Study:* Choosing to spend time meditating upon the Word of God. The goal of this discipline is not acquiring information, but allowing God to form lives spiritually.

- *Worship:* Declaring the wonder and supreme worth of God, engaging hearts, minds, soul, and body in an ongoing offering of adoration.

- *Service:* Engaging lives, resources, talents, and spiritual gifts in ministry to others.

- *Prayer:* Through the power of the Holy Spirit, communing with God through prayer and affecting the world through intercession.

- *Fellowship:* Choosing actively to integrate into the healthy, spiritual community as a place of united strength, increased faith, and demonstrated love.

Each of these disciplines can be developed to position you significantly for God's intimate presence.

Jesus invites you to enter an incredible relationship of intimacy and embrace. This relationship will be passionate, full of desire and incredible delight, and can be experienced deep within your heart. What is even more amazing is the fact that the seed of that intimacy is already within you, part of the nature of Christ that indwells every Christian. Through the nurture and nourishing process already described, that potential can grow in your life into a transforming reality.

Chapter 4

Community

I found one of the greatest treasures of my life in the last place I could have dreamed possible. The treasure was a caring community of fellow travelers. The place was Cedar Springs Psychiatric Hospital in Colorado Springs. The year 1992 was pivotal in my life and my ministry. I was experiencing a great deal of success as a Christian educator, pastor, and speaker. I served a large and growing congregation in Northern California, taught at a respectable Christian college, and was regularly sought after as a conference speaker. But just beneath the surface of my commendable public life was a sea of emotional pain and mental exhaustion. Years of driving myself had taken a toll and even my best coping skills were proving increasingly ineffective.

For several months I privately battled unusual periods of anxiety. I did everything I could to push through and stay productive. But one day everything changed. In what seemed an instant I entered a debilitating season of depression and severe agoraphobia. I could no longer work, spent months locked in emotional darkness, and became fearful even to leave my bedroom. Friends, family, and church members were shocked as they watched me wrestle with irrational fear and biochemical depression. The world I had worked so hard to create came crashing in around me. I was desperately lost.

I tried to receive help from local physicians, but the depression and agoraphobia seemed to be gaining strength. Desperate for help, I traveled to Colorado to admit myself for in-patient treatment at the Rapha Center, part of Cedar Springs Psychiatric Hospital. I will never forget standing outside the hospital that cold October day in 1992. I felt completely undone, more frightened than words could describe, and very alone in my own nightmare of mental illness. I remember crying. As far as I knew all was lost, my ministry over, and my sanity forever compromised. I did not want to pass through those double doors and enter the hospital. But desperation enabled me to put one foot in front of the other and go on a journey that was definitely not of my own choosing.

The Rapha Center was a lockdown unit. Once I passed through the main door I entered a world I had never known. The nurses checked all my possessions, took anything that could be potentially harmful, and showed me to my room. I felt desperately alone and, once again, I cried. Everyone I loved was on the other side of the locked door. My wife, my beautiful children, and my friends were out of reach. I was in a very unfamiliar place, surrounded by people who frightened me, unsure about how long I would be there or what was going to happen. I was afraid.

I ended up staying at Cedar Springs for a month, and then went to a resident aftercare facility for another two weeks. I wrote extensively about that season in *Wounded: How to Find Wholeness and Inner Healing Through Him,* and *Draw Close to the Fire: Finding God in Darkness.* It was not an easy time. There were many difficult days and painfully lonely nights. Yet, many things changed because of that difficult season. The Lord met me in amazing ways and brought good out of a bad time in my life. And the most unexpected gift that God gave me came through the other patients. By His grace I stumbled into a caring community that showed me incredible love and acceptance at a time when I questioned my very existence. They were a priceless treasure hidden in darkness.

A Caring Community

There were usually eight to ten patients on the Rapha unit while I was at Cedar Springs. They were at various points in their stay and therapeutic process, and originally came with serious personal problems. Some, like me, were battling depression and anxiety, others were there because of crippling addictions, and there were a few who were suffering from serious mental disorders. Each of us spent time daily with therapists and doctors, and formally met together as a group for various types of therapy. All that was helpful. But there was a significant amount of free time. Given that we were in a lockdown unit, there was no place to go and not a lot to do. As a result, we all spent a considerable amount of time together.

I was only at Cedar Springs a few days before I experienced an incredible degree of love and support from the other patients. Once in a while we played ping pong, occasionally watched a movie at night, often sat together in silence, but mostly we shared our stories. I would have thought, prior to being in such a place, that conversations would have been dark and depressing, focusing on the horrible trials we were all facing. My experience was not at all like that. Deep bonding occurred as we all supported one another on our individual journey through very debilitating problems. I found that my fellow patients cared when I was down, wept with me when I cried, listened intently to my story, and offered their healing presence more than their advice. I was heard, often held, and not once judged for the obvious mistakes that had contributed to my dark night. I experienced a love and acceptance I had never known. It was not a planned part of the program, but instead a genuine expression of caring and, I might add, healing community.

I grew to love my Cedar Springs friends deeply and have kept in touch with several of them over the years. I have often reflected upon my experience with them, grateful that they were there with me and for me. I have also been sad that I had to go to a psychiatric hospital to have my first taste of genuine community. My days with them served to expose the years I had spent in shallow relationships, even within the church. Those six weeks also taught me a great deal about what makes true community work and a healing power. It is obvious that being together for so much *time* in a voluntary imprisonment was a significant factor. Developing depth in community takes time, and anyone hoping to create such a spiritually transforming environment must consider that it is a serious commitment demanding a significant investment of time.

But there were other factors that made this experience so formative. We were all at the end of ourselves and *desperate* for change. Our lives were being seriously compromised and we all knew that there was no time for denial. We also knew that we could not bring about the needed change on our own. We needed *Jesus*. The Rapha Center was thoroughly Christian and every client had turned there because they knew they needed Him more than anything else. Granted, there would be skills to learn, for some medication to take, and counseling to attend. But it was clear to all that Jesus was the answer.

There was also great healing from what I call the power of *presence*. It was amazing to experience personally how much their "being there" helped. For untrained professionals, these broken people sure knew the value of silent support. I remember the peace that came upon me when someone just sat with me when days were dark and times were tough. This was directly related to the fact that they were *fellow travelers*. Each of them was on the pain-filled journey. This had a two-fold affect on the experience of community. First, there was *mutual respect*. We all understood how difficult it was to be there. And, second, no one offered quick fixes or clichés to people who were in deep pain. We all knew how unhelpful that was.

The people in Cedar Springs with me had little time for pretense. Too much was at stake, and so *openness* and *honesty* were at a premium. I sat and listened to some of the saddest stories I ever heard, shared because everyone knew that only the truth would set us free. There was anger, and tears, and great disappointment. But there was also incredible *acceptance*. Not once did I feel judged by other patients. Since we had all hit the wall in some way or another, a spirit of *humility* prevailed. That also contributed to the *patience* people showed toward one another.

They all knew that this was not going to be a quick journey to wholeness. Small *victories were celebrated*, and those who were further along the path constantly promised the rest of us that there was *hope* for us all. Things would in fact get better. Finally, I remember that the patients would not allow anyone to play the victim. They knew that adopting this stance was an invitation to long-term impris-onment. Instead they encouraged one another to *remember* who they were in Christ and take personal responsibility to grow beyond what was presently happening in their lives.

I am convinced that the Holy Spirit was at work in my Cedar Springs community. It was a very tough time for us all. But He guided us into a unity of love that was genuinely healing. The Spirit empowered the way we related to one another, the expressions of support, even the words that were said. It was one of the first times I had really experienced the church being the church. And I am sure we did not understand at the time the wonder of what was truly happening.

I remember one day sitting with several of my friends, looking out the window at all the people hurrying along their busy way. I somehow realized that there was really little difference between us on the inside and the people on the outside. They, like us, were deeply wounded and probably struggling with deep inner pain. They were probably lonely, needing a safe place to experience love, and grace, and genuine care. I was sure they needed more of Jesus, just as we did. Staring out that window I somehow felt privileged. God had mercifully allowed me to find something in a psychiatric hospital that I had not been experiencing in the local church. He gave me the gift of a caring, healing community. I left Cedar Springs still in significant pain and with many unanswered questions. But this I knew. People were made for community.

The Desire for Community

Genuine community is essential for personal growth and ongoing healing. The need for community is part of our original DNA as human beings. Every person on the face of the earth would greatly benefit from meeting with a small group of people who commit to the following characteristics I experienced at Cedar Springs:

- Christ-centeredness
- Time

- Urgency
- Presence
- Common experience
- Mutual respect
- Openness
- Honesty
- Acceptance
- Grace
- Humility
- Patience
- Celebration
- Hope
- Responsibility
- The ministry of the Holy Spirit

Christians who are at all concerned about becoming like Jesus, must know this: there are some aspects of spiritual maturity that can only be developed within a caring Christian community. There is no other way. Even Jesus knew this, reflected in the depth of His commitment to be united with other people on the Christian journey. He experienced community, modeled community, and commanded community to all who would follow Him.

Jesus Christ and the Call to Community

Jesus experienced community before time began. He is eternally part of the Trinity, the divine community of Father, Son, and Spirit that is mysteriously united, yet distinct in person. Much of this is beyond our comprehension, but one thing we do know: our God, who is Three in

One, engages in constant expressions of communal life within the Trinity. Everything you could imagine about love, celebration, joy, and wonder occurs within the Divine Community. The Trinity is mutually supportive, infinitely self-giving, unfathomably creative, and eternally satisfying.

The Godhead did not create people because of loneliness. God exists in eternal fellowship. He creates because it is in His nature to create and He made humans beings so that they could participate in the glorious dance already experienced within the Trinity. Jesus came into this world from the perfect expression of community and gave His life so that we who were lost could be eternally embraced in the family of God. Jesus forever exists within community and calls His own to participate in that same expression of divine life. A person who claims to be a follower of Christ is by nature a person committed to community. Granted, that commitment may need to be developed. But Christianity is all about a people united together under the Lordship of Jesus Christ.

The Gospels reveal two important facts about the Lord's commitment to community. First, He was Himself thoroughly committed to community while on earth. At His birth a community of very different people gathered at the manger to receive Him into the world. Mary and Joseph were joined by angels and shepherds and kings from the East. They worshiped the Christ-child and rejoiced in the wonder of His dear, sweet life. Jesus also grew in community, spending His life as part of a real family with parents, brothers and sisters. He was also part of a small town and I am sure a participating member of a local synagogue. Far from isolated, Jesus was integrated into the fabric of Jewish society, identified by His place within the clan, tribe, and nation. Matthew begins his Gospel by placing Jesus within the history of His people (Matthew 1:1–17).

When Jesus began His earthly ministry He called specific men to join Him as disciples and co-workers (Mark 1:14–20). He formed a community around Himself that would eventually carry on His work following His return to heaven. For three years Jesus invested His time, and love, and power into their lives. He taught them principles of the Kingdom, gave them authority to heal and deliver people from darkness, and empowered them to work signs and wonders. They lived together, traveled throughout the region ministering to the hurting together, and preached the gospel wherever they went. At times great crowds followed Jesus, but it was His community of twelve that received the focus of much of His attention.

There were important events that they shared together, especially during the Passion of the Lord. Jesus was with His community at the triumphal entry into Jerusalem (Luke 19:28–44), in the upper room during the Passover (John 13), and during the agony of Gethsemane (Mark 14:32–42). His community was there at His arrest (Mark 14:43–51), close by at the trial (Matthew 26:57–75), and at least a few were present at Golgotha (John 19:25–27). Jesus appeared to His gathered community on several occasions following the resurrection (John 20:19–21, 26). And on the day He ascended into heaven they were all there, except the betrayer, to receive final instructions and see Jesus disappear in the clouds (Matthew 28:16–20). Jesus cared deeply for the individual person, yet prioritized community as the best context for growth and ministry. A genuine commitment to Christ has always involved a commitment to His community. There is not one without the other.

Second, Jesus taught His disciples many Kingdom principles. Matthew records a very important set of instructions that emphasize the critical nature of community. Jesus told the disciples that if a person sinned against another, the offended person should go privately to the brother and show him his fault. If the brother refused to listen, the person offended should take two or three others and confront him again. If he still refused to respond appropriately, the matter should be referred to the church, the gathering of Christ's followers (Matthew 18:15–17). Jesus said that there was great power available to followers who were united in Christ's name (Matthew 18:18–19). Jesus then went on to promise disciples of all time that wherever as few as two or three people gathered in His name, He would be there with them (Matthew 18:20). True Christian community is a place that promises power, authority, and the presence of Christ.

Luke records an important story regarding community in chapter 10. Jesus sent seventy-two followers into the towns and villages that He would later visit. It is instructive that Jesus sent them two by two. Ministry occurred within a small intimate community of two people dedicated to the Lord and to one another. How contrary this is to the modern American emphasis on individualism and independence, a paradigm that increasingly isolates people from each other and results in loneliness and eccentricity. Jesus repeatedly demonstrated His commitment to genuine community as the context for personal growth and effective ministry.

In the upper room Jesus gave His disciples a new commandment. He told them that they were to love one another as He had loved them (John 13:34). Christ then made a statement that Christians must take to heart. He said,

"By this all men will know that you are my disciples, if you love one another." (John 13:35)

Christians must pay careful attention to this statement. According to Jesus, it is not our service, or giving, or wisdom, or even miracle-working power that speaks of our disciple-ship. It is our love for one another. Such love demands a deep commitment to be in community, demonstrating to the world that we are united in His name. How sad that there is so much division within the global Christian community and many local churches. Nothing reveals our immaturity like divisiveness and aggression so evident among Christians of the twenty-first century. Jesus was clearly dedicated to the transforming power of community. His followers must, by the power of the Holy Spirit, choose to do the same.

The Apostle Paul picked up this theme in several of his epistles. Probably the most instructive teaching on Christian community is found in 1 Corinthians 12. Paul compared the church to a body, stating that every believer, regardless of race or station in life, is an important part (vv. 12–13). He went on to write that the Holy Spirit determines which part of the body each member constitutes, and added, that no matter how seemingly small or insignificant, each part was critical to the health and mission of Christ's body (vv. 14–25). Paul also stated that Christians are to be so interrelated that if one person suffers, the whole body suffers (v. 26). Paul followed this with his incredible teaching on the nature of true love, found in 1 Corinthians 13.

Jesus commands His followers to be active participants in His community of disciples. From eternity past He has been dedicated to "life together" and will someday take us to heaven where we will be forever united as His beloved bride. Our commitment to genuine community is essential to spiritual maturity. There can be no becoming like Christ without sharing His commitment to a healthy expression of vibrant community in His name. Again, some aspects of the potential we hold within our hearts as new creations in Christ Jesus can only be realized as we faithfully meet in His name.

Granted, community will not always be easy. We are imperfect people and our imperfections can be very challenging. That was true in Jesus' community. I am sure that the disciples had to work themselves through some difficulties, given the diversity of their personalities, interests, and political ideals. But they knew that being committed to Jesus meant being committed to one another. To choose Christ is to say yes to His people. Some of us may, for good reasons, be apprehensive about participating in a caring community. We may have been hurt by people in the past. Sadly that does happen, too often.

But the call of Christ is clear. We were made for community and the seed of that desire is present within us. There are key characteristics essential to healthy community and commitments that we must make to see it work. Let us now consider several practical steps to nourishing and nurturing that aspect of Christ-likeness in order to reflect increasingly the One who has called us to follow.

Nourishment and Nurture

What does genuine Christianity community look like? Answering that question provides the starting point for responding to the command of Christ to be united in love for one another. You must realize that true Christian community means far more than being a member of a local church or participating in a small group. As important as these may be, it is possible that key characteristics of community may be missing from such gatherings of people. When that is true the transforming impact of group life is significantly limited. Remember, Christian community involves far more than simply meeting together. There are essential ingredients of life together and those must be intentionally embraced by all the members of the group. I mentioned several in the introduction to this chapter. I want to highlight six here and give more insight into them. They are:

- size
- membership
- the centrality of Christ
- the freedom of the Spirit
- grace
- encouragement

Size

The larger the size of the group the more difficult it is to create genuine Christian community. Jesus had an inner core of three and a maximum number of twelve in His close community. That provides the parameters for membership in a group dedicated to intense commitment and deep personal growth. Restricting the size allows the members to minister intentionally to one another and be more attentive to personal and group needs. It allows the members to grow deeper in their love for one another and in their response to the call of Christ upon their lives. A small group is also more likely to foster an atmosphere of safety and openness than one that is larger. These qualities are essential to developing genuine community.

Membership

Jesus was very selective about His small group. He spent a significant amount of time in prayer before choosing His disciples. He did not simply extend an open invitation to any one who may be interested. He wanted to be led of the Father in the selection process and then individually called each man to follow Him. This practice should be instructive to you when seeking to be part of a small group dedicated to community. Prayer should precede involvement. Membership is not for the faint of heart or those who are casual about their involvement. An open invitation to just anyone interested is usually a formula for shallowness and inconsistency. People who gather with you to truly experience the power of Christian community must recognize the seriousness of that commitment. It is going to take time, demand honesty, and require a level of submitting to one another and the Lord that few seem willing to embrace. Granted, it takes time to develop depth. But the vision for membership in such a group should be clear from the beginning.

The Centrality of Christ
Meeting together in Christian community is all about Jesus. He is the Treasure for which we sell all; He is the Pearl of great price. Jesus must be the very center of every person's life and every meeting. Practically, that means worshiping Him together through songs, hymns, and words of praise. Members should be encouraged to share their personal stories of being touched by Christ and celebrate His Lordship over their lives. Time should be spent learning together about Christ from the testimony of Scripture, as well as from authors who write of His wonder and power. Acts of love and ministry should be done in His name and prayers should be lifted in unity before His heavenly throne. Members should be positioned to support one another on the lifelong journey to become more like Jesus in every way. People who participate in Christian community should be Christ-possessed!

The Ministry of the Holy Spirit
John records an amazing encounter that the disciples had with Jesus following the resurrection. He stood before His

followers, breathed upon them and said, *"Receive the Holy Spirit"* (John 20:22). The Lord repeatedly told the disciples that He would give them the Holy Spirit to empower their lives for victorious living and effective ministry. This event was the grand prelude to the mighty outpouring of the Holy Spirit that would come at Pentecost. Jesus even instructed the disciples to do nothing until they had been baptized in His power (Acts 1:4–5). He knew that the presence of the Holy Spirit was essential to everything it meant to be His follower. Christians today must recognize the role the Spirit is to play in their lives. Far too often believers have sadly opted for a powerless faith that appears safe but is in fact impotent and ineffective. Too much ministry happens in human power. People who meet with you for genuine Christian community must be open to the fire of the Flame of Love. Chapter 8 focuses exclusively on the work of the Holy Spirit in the lives of God's surrendered servants.

Grace

Everything you receive from Christ flows from His grace. You do not earn His love or acceptance, nor do you deserve the countless blessings that come your way. Christianity is completely founded upon the grace of God that extends the blessings of the Kingdom to all who receive Christ as the Lord of Life. And that attitude must be reflected in the way you relate to other people. There is absolutely no room for pride or prejudice in the heart of Christ's follower. Instead, we are humbly to reckon others as better than ourselves and serve all people as though we were serving the Lord. Nowhere should the qualities of grace be more evident than in genuine Christian community. Members should seek the Spirit's help in being loving with one another, patient, and generous of heart. They should accept each other unconditionally, seeing the potential that each person holds within as the children of God.

Encouragement

The writer of Hebrews instructed Christians to meet together regularly and continually encourage one another until Christ returns (Hebrews 10:25). He was well aware that the Christian life is not easy. There are selfish forces from within and evil powers from without that work to derail believers. There will be great trials and inevitable failings. Pressing on in Christ demands that Christians support one another all along the path. Words of love and kindness go a long way, as well as gentle reminders that we belong to Christ and nothing will separate us from His love (Romans 8:39). The members of genuine Christian community must grow to see beneath the brokenness and sin in their lives to the wonder of Christ's nature that indwells them. They should encourage each other to submit to the Spirit-empowered process of perfecting, no matter how difficult or painful it may be. And they should celebrate every step along the way as movement is made toward the ultimate gift of being more like Jesus.

Are you involved in such a caring community of fellow travelers? You now know that you must be, for it is not only the way of Christ, it is the path to spiritual maturity. If you have such a community, rejoice for it is a gift from God. If you are part of a small group but it does not have the characteristics of genuine community, pray that the Lord will open the door for you to share your heart's desire. You may be the instrument God uses to refocus the group for more Christ-like purposes. It could be that you do not have a group with whom to meet. Ask the Lord to guide you to such a gathering or, by the Spirit's power, start one on your own. You could use this book as a resource. Allow prayer to guide you and I am confident that the Lord will lead your steps.

You were made for such community and some aspects of your spiritual potential will only be developed in the context of other believers. Saying yes to this command of Christ positions you to be increasingly transformed in His presence.

Chapter 5

Character

I was invited to attend a family reunion by one of the families in the church I served. I had been to several such gatherings as a pastor and anticipated that this one would be no different from the others. There would be good food, fellowship, and an opportunity to meet some new people. I thought I may even have an opportunity to invite some folks to attend our worship service. This reunion, however, is forever seared in my memory as one of the most uncomfortable days of my life.

The gathering took place at an area park on a Sunday afternoon following church services. My responsibilities at the church kept me from being there as the dinner began, but I arrived in time to join in the festivities. Everyone was seated in the outdoor pavilion enjoying their meal and talking with family and friends. I walked up to the gathering looking for the people I knew. A man rose to greet me as I approached the tables. He pleasantly introduced himself and then asked who I was.

I told him that I was an area pastor invited by a member of the family. He gently took my arm and led me over to where everyone was seated. He then got everyone's attention and said, "Folks, we have a pastor here. Hold your wallet and grab your wife!" The blood immediately rushed from my face and I could hardly take a breath. I was more than embarrassed. I was humiliated. People laughed as he walked away, leaving me standing there all alone. After what seemed to be an eternity, my friend stepped forth to show me a seat. I have no memory of when I started to breathe again. All I know was that it was one of the worst moments of my ministry.

I never knew what the man's story was, but obviously he carried some major baggage about pastors and I was guilty by association. Somewhere in the past he had encountered a pastor or pastors who did not live what they preached. That happens all too often and the problem is not isolated to Christians in professional ministry. A significant complaint from the unbelieving world is that believers do not always live lives consistent with their faith. That is certainly not true of all Christians, but there is enough evidence of this inconsistency to see that there is a serious problem with spiritual immaturity within the church.

Unchurched people want to know more than facts about the Christian life. They want to see if those beliefs really make a difference in the way Christians live. Many years ago, while in South Africa, Gandhi came under the influence of Christians. After observing their lives, Gandhi commented that he might have become a follower of Christ had he ever met a Christian who lived what they said they believed. I commented on this in class one day and had a student angrily object to what I was saying. He said, "Christianity is not about me. It is about Jesus." He then went on to state an oft-repeated cliché. "Christians are not perfect, just forgiven." Other students nodded in agreement. I told him that I saw that attitude as a cop-out to the call of Christ to be His living witness in the world. I could see that he was very uncomfortable with my response.

I believe that his reaction, not untypical of countless

others, shows a serious misunderstanding of the call to be like Christ. We are to be more than forgiven sinners. Christians are to reflect the Lord increasingly in their lives. Paul wrote in 2 Corinthians,

> *"And we, who with unveiled faces all reflect the Lord's glory, are being transformed into his likeness with ever-increasing glory, which comes from the Lord, who is the Spirit."*
>
> (2 Corinthians 3:18)

The nature of being a Christian demands an ongoing transformation into Christ's likeness and, as Paul says, that is to increase in intensity as the Holy Spirit works in our lives. There will be setbacks, we will make mistakes, and it does take time to grow. But the goal is clearly defined in Scripture. We are to become like Jesus.

More than Behavior Modification

One of the greatest problems we face as Christians is the gap that often exists between what we say and how we live. It is a serious issue, not only for individual spiritual health, but also for viable Christian witness. The evidence does suggest that many believers seem to feel some type of pressure to pretend to be something they are not. But sooner or later their true selves leak out, causing many to question the seriousness of their claims to follow Jesus. In chapter 1 I commented on the common practice there is in many churches to prioritize belief, behavior, and service. I am convinced that this significantly contributes to the problem of pretense. When a premium is placed upon certain acceptable behaviors as the standard of Christian living, people will usually try to modify their actions accordingly. They especially try to do this whenever within sight of other believers. But the real issues that people struggle with remain untouched.

I believe there are two reasons for this pretense. On the one hand, it is because people are taught that Christianity involves being obedient to a set of rules. Some are told that real Christians do not drink, or smoke, or dance, or swear, or any one of a hundred other behaviors. Desiring to follow Christ truly, people start to change the way they behave, at least in public. They want to measure up, so they cover up. But certain situations bring out the person's real issues, and the hypocrisy is out in the open.

People also clean up their acts because they do not want to face the rebuke that could result if other Christians really knew the issues they struggled with privately. People have seen how many church members react when a Christian falls, and they do not want to face the rejection. They instead hide their struggles and pretend to be better than they really are. But the personal problems remain, often intensifying because they battle alone and in the dark. And, as mentioned, the time invariably comes when the truth is exposed, which often brings shame to the person and negative critique from others. The "And you call yourself a Christian" comments begin to fly. As a result, the cycle of frustration continues as people take their struggles into hiding and pretend to be something they are not, fearing rejection and disqualification.

Behavior modification never goes deep enough to bring lasting change. More importantly, Jesus did not see it as an answer for sin and immaturity in people's lives. Jesus always emphasized character transformation, a deep work of the Holy Spirit that brings lasting change at the very core of life. Jesus does not want people to behave. He wants them to be changed, to be shaped at the level of character, not actions. He knows that behaving like a Christian does not identify a person as a Christian. That evaluation takes place at a far deeper level, at the very heart of who people really are.

Jesus invites people to be honest about their true struggles, believing that being honest is the first step to being free. Many Christians wrestle with serious personal problems, yet do so without the help of God's people. They hide beneath a cosmetic of pretense. That is sad. The church should not be a gathering of people who behave appropriately. It should be a place where it is okay for people to be open about their deepest sins and weaknesses, without fear of rebuke or rejection. Only as these issues are brought into the open can people be positioned for the transforming work of the Holy Spirit that sets them free. The Gospels clearly show that Jesus was tender toward broken people, not judgmental. He showed grace to the sinner and brought deliverance to those caught in bondage. He helped the lost find their way home and gave direction to those blinded by darkness. He did not come to condemn, but instead gave His life that others might be saved.

Jesus and Character Transformation

When I was a little boy my parents would take my sister and me to visit our great aunt and uncle who lived in Clairton, Pennsylvania. They lived in a fine house situated high on the hill that overlooked town. Uncle Ray was a kind and affectionate man, and Aunt Alice the epitome of control and propriety. She was always dressed in "church clothes" and seemed a bit stern to me as a young child. In adulthood I found her to be wonderful, one of my favorite people on earth. But as a child I found her quite imposing.

Uncle Ray and Aunt Alice's home was immaculate. It was beautifully decorated and the furniture was quite luxurious, and always covered in see-through plastic. I am not sure but that she put the covers on in anticipation of our arrival. I remember that my mother gave us clear instructions to sit on the floor, and I have a picture from 1957 with me dutifully in my assigned place on the carpet. One of the last things my mother said to me before arriving was, "Terry, you behave yourself." Mom knew that I could easily do something inappropriate, and so I was admonished to think before I acted. If I didn't, things could get uncomfortable.

For much of my life I knew that there was a significant tension between what I wanted to do and say and what I should do and say in society. I wanted to speak out and act out in ways that were simply not acceptable. I had reaped the consequences of my bad choices enough to curb my actions, but my thoughts and desires were many times at odds. Even into adulthood I often heard myself repeating my mother's words, only now it was my own inner voice speaking. "Terry, you behave yourself! Think before you act." This was true long into my walk with the Lord. I knew that many of my actual desires were unacceptable, and so I would struggle to behave.

That leads me to an important question. Did Jesus have to behave? Did He ever experience an internal tension between what He wanted to do and what He should do as a servant of God? Did Jesus fight to suppress a deep desire to rebel against what was pure and right so that He could behave appropriately? Scripture gives us the answer and it is no, no, no. Jesus was pure and spotless from the inside out (1 Peter 1:19). His nature was divine, perfectly reflecting the love, and purity, and goodness of God (Hebrews 1:3). Jesus responded naturally in life, His actions in complete harmony with His character. He did not act loving, He was loving. Jesus did not behave with kindness, He was kind. The Lord did not choose to be compassionate, His very nature was caring. What people saw in Jesus' actions was the honest reflection of who He truly was deep within. Jesus was completely holy.

The Apostle Peter wrote that through Christ God has given believers everything we need for life and godliness (2 Peter 1:3). He went on to say that through that promise we can *"participate in the divine nature and escape the corruption in the world caused by evil desires"* (2 Peter 1:4). This incredible scripture is saying that we have within us the nature of Jesus Christ. The seed of His character has been implanted within our spirits. Through Christ we can be free from the evil desires that drive people to lives of darkness and sin. Christians can move from immaturity to maturity, through the transforming work of the Holy Spirit. For example, where the immature Christian wants to steal, but doesn't because it's wrong, the mature Christian no longer has that evil desire. Where the immature Christian wants to lie, or strike out, or seek revenge, the mature Christian is naturally honest, kind, and forgiving. This change does not happen overnight. Spiritual maturation takes time. But the seed of Christ's character is within each believer and holds the potential for all to become more like Jesus.

Kingdom Character

A great crowd was following Jesus, so He went up on a mountainside, sat down, and began to teach. What He said was so unlike what they were used to hearing from the religious leaders of their day. The Pharisees and priests seemed always to be placing another behavioral burden upon the people. Their teachings were about externals, delivered with stern warnings and the promise of judgment. But Jesus was talking to them about matters of the heart.

He started by speaking about several heart attitudes that would be found in true Kingdom people. Jesus spoke of poverty of spirit, inner sorrow, humility, and spiritual hunger. He lifted up mercy, purity, peacemaking, and faithfulness. He even talked about having joy in the midst of persecution and insult, assuring the listeners that every one of these qualities was precious in the eyes of God and would not go unrewarded (Matthew 5:12).

Jesus then told the crowd that people with these heart attitudes are the salt of the earth. He said that people like this are the light of the world and should simply allow that light to shine and, in the end, others will actually be able to see God better from the light (Matthew 5:13–16).

The people of that time found it hard to follow all the religious laws that had been placed upon them. Jesus took the discussion to a much deeper level. He said that the real issue rests with the state of the human heart. He told them that it was not enough not to murder a person. He said that even to hold hatred in the heart was wrong (Matthew 5:21–22). Jesus said the same thing about adultery. It is not enough, according to Jesus, simply to say no to the act of marital unfaithfulness. Even to lust in the heart is sinful and must be dealt with at that level (Matthew 5:27–30).

Repeatedly that day Jesus spoke at a level far deeper than rules and regulations. He told His followers that Kingdom people are different inside. They do not strike back when offended; they give generously to those in need; they love even their enemies, and pray for the very people that are attacking them. Jesus condemned the practice of making a public show of one's religious acts, telling them that Kingdom people pray, and give, and serve in secret. They do not fast for public recognition or desire worldly wealth. They have learned to trust the Lord in all things, believing that their loving Father will provide everything they need (Matthew 6:1–32).

Jesus told His followers that Kingdom people keep their

eyes on the Kingdom and seek a righteousness that goes far beyond rules. He said that such people do not judge others for their failings, but instead focus upon their own sin and immaturity. They seek the Father's help, keep their eyes open for false prophets, and prioritize their relationship with Christ. Jesus concluded by saying that the people who live like this will stand up under the worst of times. Others, who live to obey external rules, will someday be washed away like a house built upon the sand (Matthew 6:33–7:27).

The listeners were stunned by what Jesus said (Matthew 7:28). They had never heard teaching like this, spoken with such authority and authenticity. They were used to listening to the Pharisees who were self-righteous and disingenuous. Their words did not match their actions, and no matter how hard they tried to cover up with robes and titles, their shallow lives were exposed for all to see. Earlier I commented on how tender Jesus was with broken people. Not so in His attitude toward the religious leaders of that day. He openly chastised them for being hypocrites, for pretending to be more than they truly were. Jesus exposed them as religious frauds, calling them whitewashed tombs, blind guides, and a brood of vipers.

Mark records a confrontation that Jesus had with the Pharisees, when they became incensed that the disciples were not "behaving" properly. Jesus told them that the real issue for people is character, not behavior. He said that it is the inside of a person that determines whether they are clean or unclean, not obedience to religious externals (Mark 7:1–23). Probably Jesus' most stinging evaluation of the Pharisees is recorded in Matthew 23. He exposed the religious leaders as men who were in love with their own importance. They wore long robes, insisted upon the best seats at banquets, reveled in important titles, and led people astray with their teachings. Jesus said that they were preoccupied with unnecessary externals that were meaningless. Jesus chastised them for shutting the way of the Kingdom in people's faces, and warned religious leaders to pay more attention to character than behavior (Matthew 23).

How different the Pharisees were from the people Jesus was describing in the Sermon on the Mount. Surely His words left people wondering, "Could people really live like those Jesus described?" Does anyone have that kind of heart? The fact is, on our own it is absolutely impossible. It would take a radical transformation at the very core of a person's being. And that is precisely what Jesus knew. The Sermon on the Mount is not a list of behaviors that Christians are to adopt. It is a description of Kingdom living that only happens when a person allows Jesus to transform the heart by the power of the Holy Spirit. Jesus delivered the sermon to show that God's standard of righteousness is far beyond religious rules and regulations. Kingdom people are to live according to a much higher standard. It is so demanding that only a transforming act of grace could enable a person to reach that level of spiritual maturity. And that is what being a new creation in Christ Jesus is all about.

Paul and Christian Character

Paul challenged believers to live according to the Spirit who is present within their lives (Romans 8:4). He said that Christians do not need to be controlled by the old sinful nature. The Holy Spirit who raised Christ from the dead is present within them to put to death all those misdeeds (Romans 8:9–13). Paul was telling believers that, because of Christ, they can mature to the place where they no longer struggle with the tension between what they want to do and what they should do. They can be free from the pressure to pretend to be something they are not. Jesus has given believers His nature, and Christians can now behave according to the character of Christ within.

In several epistles Paul listed the kind of sinful behaviors that grow out of the sinful nature. They include things such as sexual immorality, impurity, lust, evil desires, greed, anger, rage, malice, filthy language, lying, and slander (Colossians 3:5–10). Paul told believers that these dead works grieve the Holy Spirit and were inconsistent with the new nature that Jesus had placed within them (Ephesians 4:20–32). According to Paul the Holy Spirit is present to help believers move beyond these weakness to spiritual maturity (Romans 8:26–27).

Paul also described what life looks like when lived from the divine nature that indwells believers. He stated that the new Christ-like self produces love, joy, peace, patience, kindness, goodness, faithfulness, gentleness, and self-control. He called these the fruit of the Spirit, the natural outcome of an inner life that reflects Jesus Christ (Galatians 5:22). He went on to say that people who live by the Spirit do not continually struggle with the old desires to sin. Those who belong to Christ have crucified those passions and now live in step with the Holy Spirit (Galatians 5:16–24). Paul was speaking here about the spiritually mature, people who have allowed the Holy Spirit to transform their lives, nourishing and nurturing the seed of Christ's character that has made them new creations.

Nourishment and Nurture

I am confident that the Holy Spirit desires to bring you to spiritual maturity. Jesus gave His blood to make that possible and, if willing, you can experience that transforming work. As has already been stated, this is a process and it does take time. But the fruit of change will soon be evident in your heart if you say yes to the Holy Spirit. The nature of Christ begins to grow and you will increasingly reflect the nature of Jesus Christ. That is to His glory.

Christian character is an essential part of spiritual maturity. Far too many believers do not understand this concept and wrestle with feelings of hypocrisy. They secretly recognize that there is a dangerous distance between what they say as Christians and how they live. Eventually that inconsistency is exposed, which compromises their witness to those outside the body of Christ. Jesus has provided a way for that to be changed. The invitation of Christ to you is the call to maturity. I am going to suggest several ways in which you can be positioned for that transforming work of the Holy Spirit.

1. First, lay claim to the fact that the seed of His nature is already present in your life. You are not missing something that is key to your victory. Scripture promises that because of Christ you already have all you need to live a godly life (Ephesians 1:3). The fruit of the Spirit mentioned earlier is present within you, and simply needs to be nourished and nurtured to bring forth good. The evil one may try to discourage you, accuse you of being a fake, and work to convince you that you are a bad person. That is all a lie. Jesus has given you His nature and you are a loved child of God. Lay hold of that truth and do not let it go.

2. Second, regularly read the word of God, allowing the Holy Spirit to guide you into all truth. After Paul told the Colossian church to put off the old self, he encouraged them to allow God's word to dwell in their hearts, richly (Colossians 3:16). Scripture is the inspired word of God and it will produce fruit in those who read it with an open heart. Christians of the past practiced a spiritual discipline called "the antirrhetic method." That is a fancy term for

memorizing scriptures that correspond to specific needs in your life. If you struggle with hate, memorize texts on love. If you struggle with selfishness, meditate on biblical teachings about servanthood and generosity. The concept is simple but, under the guidance of the Holy Spirit, the result can be profound. The writer of Hebrews said that God's word is sharper than a double-edged sword, able to go to the very heart of a person (Hebrews 4:12). That is the place where real change happens.

3. Third, daily ask the Holy Spirit to search your life for sin and inconsistencies. King David believed that God was intimately aware of everything about us. He said that there was nothing we could ever do, and nowhere we could ever go that God was not present. David said that God knew what we were going to say before it even came out of our mouths. At the end of Psalm 139 he wrote,

> *"Search me, O God, and know my heart;*
> *test me and know my anxious thoughts.*
> *See if there is any offensive way in me,*
> *and lead me in the way everlasting."*
>
> (Psalm 139:23–24)

This must be our constant prayer. God is thoroughly familiar with you. But He will not force His will upon your life. He has given you the right to choose the level of involvement He is to have in your spiritual development. I encourage you to ask Him to turn on the searchlight of the Holy Spirit. Allow Him to deal with any inconsistencies between what you believe and how you live. It may not be painless, but you will rejoice as the seed of Christ's character grows in your life.

4. Fourth, regularly practice the discipline of confession. When David finally stopped hiding his sin with Bathsheba,

he went to God and confessed what he had done (Psalm 51). He admitted that he had strayed from God and asked for cleansing and forgiveness. God was merciful and David was restored. Jesus has made a way for you that is beyond words. Through the cross all your sin, past, present, and future has been cleansed before God. Your standing as His child is in place and your inheritance is secure. But it is still necessary that you confess your sins. Confession is a discipline of agreement. It is your prayerful recognition that there are specific areas of your life that do not reflect your new nature in Jesus Christ. By agreeing, you position yourself for the Spirit's transforming touch in those immature places.

5. Fifth, learn to surrender all of your life to God as part of His transforming work. Paul stated that God intended to see all Christians mature into the image of Christ (Romans 8:29). The scripture verse prior to that tells us how that is going to happen. The Lord will use "all things" toward that purpose, if we allow Him to. That means everything we do and all things that happen to us, be they good or bad, happy or sad. The Apostles Paul, Peter, and James each said that trials are part of God's plan (Romans 5:3–5; James 1:2–4; 1 Peter 1:6–7). Many believers would like to ignore that fact, hoping to live problem-free lives as a reward for following Jesus. That is an immature and unbiblical attitude. Throughout the history of the Church Christians have said that difficulties nurture Christian character. That is true if and when believers offer those trials to the Lord for His perfecting process. Those who do ultimately meet the Lord in new and powerful ways.

6. Sixth, character is nourished and nurtured within genuine Christian community. I have already discussed this principle at length in the previous chapter. The Holy Spirit moves among the gathered people of God. And as He does, people are changed. Anyone who reads the New Testament

can see that this is true, particularly when considering the disciples. They went from a ragtag group of misfits to a powerful force for the gospel in the ancient world. They were transformed from selfishness to selflessness as they gathered together in Jesus' name. To one degree or another that always happens in genuine Christian community. Character is called forth and matured as believers come together to worship, learn, pray, and serve. You need that experience of shared life, for it is the atmosphere that best nurtures and nourishes the seed of Christ in your life.

There is a powerful prophecy given at the end of the book of Zechariah. The prophet is looking into the future and he sees a day when people from ten different nations will lay their hands upon the cloak of a child of God and say, *"Let us go with you, because we have heard that God is with you"* (Zechariah 8:23). May the Holy Spirit of Jesus Christ make that true in your life.

Chapter 6

Brokenness

Since 1992 I have spent hundreds of hours helping people find healing from deep emotional wounds. I have listened to countless stories of rejection and abuse that have been unimaginable, told by people who appeared on the surface to be together in every way. Most of their friends would have no idea that something traumatic had happened to them. The wounded have learned to hide what is ugly, put on a happy face, and try to get on with life. This helps them feel safe and they think it protects them from further wounding. But deep inside they battle an incredible degree of pain from wounds usually caused by those closest to them. Many have tried to put what happened behind them. They have learned some coping skills that help alleviate some of the pain, at least enough to have a relatively normal life, and they have tried to forget. For a while that seems to work. But sooner or later the pain becomes too much to bear, and breakdown begins.

Sadly, some people, like my friend Garrett, were abused before they ever left their mothers' wombs. Garrett battles tremendous fear, which is ultimately rooted in His mother's attempts to self-abort during pregnancy. Other individuals have experienced varying degrees of trauma in infancy or childhood. That is what happened to Sharon. Her father would come home in a drunken rage and beat her and her brother for just being alive. I have also listened to adults speak of severe wounding during adolescence, like Connie who spent years hiding the truth about her sexual abuse at the hands of a neighbor. And more people than I can count were wounded as adults, just like Jennifer, who spent years listening to her husband scream at her, hurling abusive words that deeply scarred her sense of worth.

Most people in our society have experienced some level of emotional trauma. Either they did not receive the love and care they should have, or they unfortunately received painful abuse they were never meant to endure. The wounds people receive vary in type, frequency and intensity. But regardless of what happened, the pain is real and deep and has had a lasting impact upon their lives. Few in our society understand the seriousness of emotional wounding. Unaddressed, it can cause physical, psychological, relational, and spiritual distress. People can lose their health, their loved ones, and their sanity because of the inappropriate ways in which they try to kill the pain of deep wounding.

It is my experience that many Christian leaders do not understand emotional wounding. When people turn to them for help, Christian leaders tend to offer pious platitudes and clichés that are insensitive and demeaning. I myself experienced that when struggling with depression and agoraphobia. I remember sharing what was happening with a pastor who was a friend. He listened to my story and then said, "Terry, where's your faith?" I cannot describe the anger that I felt inside at that moment. My story is far from isolated. That is why a lot of people do not turn to the church for help with emotional pain. They fear being misunderstood, judged, or worst of all discounted.

Christians must learn to deal with deep emotional wounding. Few have been spared and many are responding to what happened in the past in ways that will ultimately bring greater pain and heartache. As with all things, I want to show that Jesus alone provides the pathway to deep healing for the emotionally wounded. But, first, I want to share Jason's story. It is not atypical of what happens to someone when significantly abused. It also provides a framework of understanding deep emotional trauma.

An All-too-familiar Story

When I first met Jason he was dressed in women's clothing and went by the name Janet. He had been befriended by a member of the church I pastored and was brought to our growth group. He was not a small person and even behind all the clothes and makeup everyone knew that "Janet" was really a guy. The members of the group received him lovingly and over time proceeded to win him to Christ. Slowly changes began to take place and in time Jason was dressing like a man and beginning to grow as a new believer.

But Jason was struggling at many levels. He had a terrible time in crowds, smoked one cigarette after another, would often arrive with alcohol on his breath, and could not hold down a job. He was very awkward socially, which caused a lot of people in the church to keep him at a distance. Those that did get close to Jason were amazed at how intelligent he was, while at the same time aware that he acted far more like an insecure teenager than a man in his mid-forties. Whenever Jason did get close to someone he would latch on in ways that were almost smothering, relating to them as though they were required to care for his every need. When people set boundaries with Jason he would overreact, claim that they really did not care about him, and step away from the relationship.

Most everyone in our church knew how Jason acted. But

no one knew his story. But that story held the key to his broken life. Time and circumstance provided the window of opportunity. Jason initially shared his story with a woman in the church and gave her permission to tell me. What I learned was heartbreaking and brought all Jason's dysfunctional ways into clear focus.

Jason wanted people to know that he was not gay. His cross-dressing was driven by an irrational fear of men, not sexual confusion. He told my friend that he was the oldest child of eight, raised by an abusive father. His mother had left when he was a child, never to be seen or heard from again. His dad was an alcoholic. He would often leave the children at home alone, instructing Jason to watch them, with the warning that if anything went wrong he alone would be punished.

Jason said that countless times his father would return and be upset about something, anything, and begin to beat Jason severely. He would punch Jason with his fist, beat him with belts, lock him in closets, and refuse him food. If any of the children were hurt, or if something broke while he was away or seemed out of order, Jason would pay. It never mattered whether he had done it or not. Jason's dad said that he was teaching him responsibility. And so all his father's wrath was vented upon Jason.

Jason was only ten years old when this began to happen, abuse that continued in various forms until he was thrown out of the home in his late teens. By adolescence Jason was developing serious emotional problems, which affected his school work and isolated him from other kids his age. He said that any form of anger from people paralyzed him. Most of all he was terrified of men. After a series of personal failures Jason made his way to San Francisco. He got involved in drugs, was arrested several times, and essentially became a homeless wanderer. It was there that he began to cross-dress, an irrational response to the fear he had about men. In many ways he was hoping to find acceptance from women, most likely a dysfunctional response to his deep need for a mother who would come and rescue him from all the abuse.

Looking Beneath the Surface

Like all emotional problems there was an identifiable and important pattern to what was happening in Jason's life. Discovering that pattern has been very helpful in my own healing and that of the hundreds of people I have worked with through the years. I have written extensively about this process of inner healing in my book *Healing Care, Healing Prayer*. There, I identify the layers of emotional difficulty as similar to the layers of an onion. First, at the outer layer is the person's *life situation*. This is the specific context in which a person lives and experiences personal conflict. When I met Jason his life situation was unemployment, transition to a new community, and homelessness, each an extremely difficult and stress-producing matter. Obviously there were important issues to be addressed here for Jason, including having money, friends to support him, and a place to live. But, as important as these matters were, solving these problems would not be enough. Jason needed deeper healing.

The second layer is that of *dysfunctional behavior*. People who met Jason when he first entered our fellowship could readily see that he had problems. They saw his clothes, his chain-smoking, and his socially awkward behavior, and easily concluded that he needed help. What he was doing was physically, emotionally, spiritually, and relationally damaging. Unaddressed Jason could die an early death, alone and desperately lost. Jason needed help and it would take a power far greater than himself to ultimately experience healing and freedom.

Not all dysfunctional behavior is as readily seen or as socially unacceptable as Jason's. Many people battle in secret, struggling with a wide variety of emotional painkillers, such as sexual addictions, drug and alcohol problems, eating disorders, and the like. These behaviors are destructive, initially promising peace yet all the while compromising personal wellbeing and mental health. Some dysfunctional behaviors are even applauded in society, such as performance addictions and people pleasing. People who embrace these behaviors masquerade as diligent workers and very friendly, accommodating individuals. But the truth is far less noble. They are dysfunctional attempts to deal with deep issues that seldom come into the light of God's healing touch.

People adopt dysfunctional behaviors to kill pain and/or meet deep personal need. Why did Jason cross-dress, chain-smoke, and act strange when around people? Because he was living in constant *emotional upheaval*. That is the third layer of the emotional onion. Jason battled chronic anxiety, was afraid of men, and felt desperately alone and unloved. Those feelings were powerful and he tried, through very dysfunctional means, to silence that pain. Much of what he did was irrational, but the emotional storm was so great that he would do absolutely anything to find a moment of internal peace.

Of course, what Jason did only made problems worse. And so it is with all dysfunctional behaviors. They are hopeless attempts to kill emotional pain. They are embraced by those who feel unreasonable fear, anxiety, loneliness, worthlessness, and shame. Such choices can also be driven by feelings of rejection, self-contempt, and abandonment. These are powerful emotional forces that can bring great pain. So much so that people will embrace even the most destructive of behaviors to still that inner emotional storm.

If dysfunctional behaviors are driven by the power of inner emotional upheaval, what causes all the bad feelings? Beneath the layer of emotional upheaval in Jason's life was a layer I call *False Belief*. Deep inside, Jason believed that he was totally unsafe, unlovable, and at fault for the problems he had as a child. He believed that if he had been better, stronger, or more responsible, he could have been accepted by his father and loved by his mother. He also believed that all men were unsafe and positioned to hurt him. These false beliefs were hidden deep within Jason, yet they generated a tremendous amount of emotional pain, which he in turn tried to deal with through dysfunctional behaviors.

Virtually all Christians I have ever counseled or prayed with believe lies about themselves, their world, and their God. I include myself in that number. Deep below the surface of my public ministry were several false beliefs that were eating away at my life. One of the most destructive was that I had to perform well in order to be loved. That caused me great anxiety, which I tried to still by being a workaholic. I have heard God's people admit that they believed they were defective, worthy of shame, unimportant, stupid, and worthless. People have told me in private that they were convinced that they would never measure up, were a disappointment to God, and were deserving of punishment. Not one of these statements is true, yet they generate incredible power when embraced deep within the heart. Such lies cause great emotional storms that people work hard to still in very destructive and dysfunctional ways.

Beneath the dysfunctional behaviors, emotional upheaval, and false beliefs in Jason's life was the painful core, *deep wounds*. The amount of abuse and abandonment that he had experienced defies adequate description. He was beaten, raged at, locked in closets, and punished for things that were not his responsibility. These wounds left physical scars, but the greatest injury occurred deep within his spirit. Jason's parents had broken him severely. These wounds were at the center of all his problems. Everything Jason believed about himself, his world, and his God was shaped by these tragic events. His wounds caused him to believe that he was all alone in life and unsafe, which created great emotional turmoil, that Jason tried to calm with dysfunctional behaviors acted out in his own life situation.

While what happened to Jason is severe, the pattern is the same for all people locked in emotional problems. Deep wounds are at the core of a several-layered cause-and-effect relationship between false beliefs, emotional upheaval, dysfunctional behaviors, and life situations. Christian people are not immune to this most serious dilemma. Counselors, many of whom are Christian, attempt to make things better for people. Unfortunately, they more often than not do not go to the deeper levels where the real power lies. As a result, solutions are only mildly effective, helping people limp where they previously crawled.

Does Jesus have anything to say about this problem? Is there more than "better" available to hurting people? How does this matter of emotional disorder relate to spiritual maturity? Once again we turn to the life and ministry of Christ and find that even with this issue the invitation is to become more like Jesus.

Jesus and Emotional Wounding

The writer of Hebrews stated that Jesus is sympathetic with our struggles because He was tried in every way we are (Hebrews 4:15–16). Is that true in the area of wounding and abuse? The answer is an unqualified yes! Reading the Gospels reveals that Jesus not only understood emotional wounding, but He experienced it, beginning with His birth.

We know that Joseph did not initially believe Mary's story about carrying God's child. He thought that Mary had been unfaithful and determined to end their relationship. Could that tension between Mary and Joseph have had any effect on the Christ-child? I raised this question in my doctoral class on formational counseling and several students were vehement that Jesus was the Son of God and, therefore, not impacted by such issues, either in or out of the womb. I disagree. While I admit that we have no knowledge about how this matter affected Jesus, this I do know: Jesus lived His life on earth as fully human. He experienced life as we do, not as God does. That is the entire point of the incarnation. Therefore, proposing such questions is far from ridiculous. I see it as quite relevant to life as we all know it.

As an infant Christ was hunted down by Herod's killers and his parents fled with him to another land. I know several people from the third world who experienced similar trauma in childhood and they invariably struggle with fear and feelings of being unsafe. Did Jesus? I don't know. But of this I am confident; Jesus understands rejection and abuse because He experienced it. The story of Jesus continually points to emotional wounding. His siblings misunderstood Him, His community rejected His ministry, and the religious leaders hated Him. Ultimately He was betrayed by a friend, abandoned by those closest to Him, arrested and handed over to be crucified. Jesus was spat upon, slapped, whipped, stripped naked, and brutally killed. Did Jesus experience deep emotional trauma? Absolutely.

Jesus and Emotional Wholeness

With that said, we now consider what is most amazing about Jesus, the Son of Man. Unlike us, He did not embrace false beliefs as a result of all this. There is no evidence that

He felt unloved, rejected, defective, or unwanted. Jesus also showed no signs of emotional upheaval. On the contrary, He walked this earth in peace and confidence, extending love and acceptance to every broken person who came His way. Jesus also did not embrace dysfunctional behaviors. He was not a drunkard, was sexually pure, did not push people away or try to please them. Jesus, greatly wounded, was also completely healthy and whole.

Now we come to the key question of this entire discussion. Why did all this abuse not lead to serious problems for Jesus? What did He do with all the emotional rejection that He experienced? The answer is provided in Scripture from the Passion narrative about Jesus in the Garden of Gethsemane. I believe it provides an important window into how Jesus dealt with difficult emotional issues. I am suggesting that what we see Jesus do there was a pattern He had learned and practiced long before Passion Week.

Jesus was about to be betrayed, abandoned, and brutally crucified. The Gospel of Luke records that Jesus prayed so intensely that He sweat drops of blood (Luke 22:44). Jesus had hoped that His followers would support Him in this hour, but they fell asleep. So Jesus poured out His heart alone before God, grieving all that was about to happen to Him, the severest of human abuse. Three times He went to prayer asking the Father to provide a way out for Him. But somewhere in the midst of the agony, Jesus rose up with the entire matter settled in His heart. He had heard from God and would walk forward toward the cross. At Calvary Jesus brought cleansing to all sinners, forgave those who crucified Him, and promised a believing thief that paradise was his.

I am convinced that this one important event provides us with a clear picture of how Jesus dealt with deep wounding. First, He turned His eyes to the Father, not to those who had abused and rejected Him. He knew that God alone held the power to set people free and give them the strength to walk through difficult places. Second, Jesus told the Father about what was bothering Him. No one can read the account of Gethsemane and wonder what Jesus was dealing with that night. He was asking the Father for help, for human abuse was about to bring its worst to bear upon Him.

Third, Jesus grieved. He did not vent to His friends, though He had hoped for their prayer support. Nor did He spew venom at those who were positioned to hurt Him. Jesus cried out to God, expressing His emotions upward instead of outward, telling the Father exactly what He was feeling deep inside. Lamenting is part of Jewish tradition. The Psalms include the cries of abused people, and Jesus was part of that religious heritage. There in Gethsemane He poured out His inner emotional pain to the Father. The grieving was so intense that Jesus' sweat glands burst and blood began to pour down His face. His grief was real, and deep, and presented to the Father as a sacred invitation for Him to help Jesus in His hour of need.

Fourth, somewhere in the midst of this hour of prayer Jesus heard God speak and the matter was settled. He embraced the truth that the cross was His destiny and He moved forward to die as a sacrifice for sin. Prayer in Gethsemane prepared Jesus to stay the course and fulfill His mission. He knew what God expected of Him and Jesus did not waiver or fall back from God's will. Fifth, Jesus forgave those that crucified Him. He had taught His disciples about the power of forgiveness and now, after meeting with God, He extended His love to those that killed Him. Gethsemane helped Jesus forgive His killers. Jesus had grieved openly, received the Father's love, was empowered by His presence, and was now able to bless at a time when others would have called down fire. Jesus died there that day, hanging from a cruel cross as people continued to hurl abuse at Him. But He

was the victor, not them. And all eternity will show that
Jesus rose above the wounds that people caused, to reign
eternally at the right hand of God on High.

Nourishment and Nurture

There is healing for the emotionally broken and Jesus has
provided the way. Once again, we begin with the promise
that the seed of Christ has been implanted within you. That
seed holds the potential for Christ-likeness and by nourishing and nurturing that divine nature, you will grow toward
spiritual maturity, becoming more and more like Jesus.
The issue at hand is that of deep brokenness. Virtually all
Christian people have been deeply wounded in life.
Granted, there are many who would deny that things of
the past have had any real effect upon them. My response is
to consider the law of fruit and root. If there is the fruit of
dysfunction, there is the root of deep wounding. It's that
simple.

 Consider Jason. His dysfunctional behavior made it crystal
clear that there was deep wounding in His life. No matter
how hard he may have tried to hide it from others, he was a
broken man who needed the healing power of Christ at the
core of his being. That also holds true for people who are
addicted to alcohol, drugs, sex, and food. As well as those
who are trapped in people-pleasing, and performance. Where
there is great anxiety, people-pleasing, anger, phobias, and
the drive to control, there is usually false belief and deep
wounding. The pattern is there in many Christians. Broken
believers are trapped in a destructive pattern which eventually destroys much of what is good in their lives.

 Jesus, our broken friend and brother, has provided a way
to healing. Through the power of the Holy Spirit you can
respond to past, present, and future wounding as He did,

experiencing the healing power of God in the places of deepest pain. How? You must follow the steps of Gethsemane. First, always take your pain to the Father. God alone holds the power to set you free from the effects of deep wounding. Counseling can be helpful, but God alone heals. While conversations with a professional may bring some relief, talking honestly to God is transforming. When remembering past hurt, or dealing with present wounding, let prayer be the first place you go and the place you stay the longest. You may want some friends to be there for support. But God alone holds the answer.

Second, tell God exactly what happened to you, no holds barred. Be specific in prayer, even relying upon the Holy Spirit to help you remember details of the event. I remember doing this with Jason. He was hesitant at first, but I persisted, encouraging him to be open and honest before the throne. Soon Jason was able to tell his story to God, just as it happened. This led him into the third and most important part of the process. Jason began to grieve. There was an ocean of pain and heartache inside, stuffed away for years. But as he told God about what happened, the tears, and anger, and fear began to surface. He was releasing a reservoir of darkness that had been dammed up in his life since childhood. It was not quick or easy, but the grieving was essential and ultimately good. You must also let your lament be heard. You may want to write a psalm and pray it aloud to God, just like the Israelites did centuries ago. If you do, be sure to be honest, allowing your feelings to be expressed openly before Him.

Fourth, listen for the whispers of God. Somewhere in the midst of the Gethsemane night Jesus heard God speak, and He was able to rise up in new strength. God still does that today, especially for the emotionally wounded who turn to Him for help. I especially encourage you to ask God how *He* feels about you. Allow His truth to penetrate into the dark recesses of your heart where old lies gain their dark strength. Emotional wounds are the breeding ground for false beliefs. Many who have been abused believe they are worthless, defective, unlovable, and worthy of punishment. But none of that is at all true for Christians. Believers are precious to God and esteemed as His own children. Scripture says that He desires to lavish love upon you. If you doubt that, ask Him in prayer. God will respond. He may answer you through Scripture, or a deep inner voice, or even a scene or picture in your imagination. One thing is sure, if the voice you hear is God's, it will be full of love and delight, assuring you that you are a priceless treasure.

Fifth, there comes a time when, like Jesus, you will need to forgive. Jesus, having grieved in Gethsemane, was able to forgive from the cross. Trying to forgive before grieving is difficult. But once the matter has been cried out honestly before the Lord, forgiveness must be extended to those who have offended you. This does not at all mean that what they did does not matter, for it does. Nor is forgiveness permission for the offender to have another chance to wound your heart. You have every right to keep distance from abusers. You are just not permitted to allow hatred to reign in your spirit. Unforgiveness will imprison you in bars of bitterness and anger. Jesus wants you free. Jesus has eternally forgiven you of all your sin. And He calls you to be like Him. Forgiveness is the way of Christ, and you are His follower, empowered to be like Him.

Finally, in the strength of Christ you are to walk in the victory that He has provided. The cross may be a symbol of defeat for some, but for believers it is the place of healing. It holds the promise of freedom, and it is the symbol of eternal victory. Through Calvary you have received the nature of Jesus and the Holy Spirit seeks to transform you daily into

His glorious likeness. You must lay claim to that glorious hope by faith, declaring even into the heavenlies that every part of your life, past, present, and future, belongs to Jesus Christ the King. And what can be more exciting, than allowing Jesus so to touch the places of deep wounding in your life that they now become a channel of healing ministry to others. Nothing could be more glorifying to God and exalting to Christ, the eternal Wounded Healer.

Chapter 7

Ministry

Jesus had gathered His disciples for one last supper, in an upper room somewhere in Jerusalem. He knew that betrayal, arrest, and trial were mere hours away, and that with the sunrise would come His death. Final instructions were critical, as were parting expressions of His deepest love. Jesus had spent three years investing in a small band of simple men, and now the responsibility to spread the gospel of the Kingdom throughout the world was falling to them. The future was in their hands. Jesus wanted them to understand clearly the true nature of the ministry that He was giving them. He knew that they still believed that they were going to overthrow the existing government and take up positions of authority under Jesus' kingship. That night Jesus showed them that ministry in His Kingdom would be very different from what they expected.

They were all seated around the table as preparations were being made for them to eat. Suddenly Jesus rose, took off His outer garment, and wrapped a towel around His waist. He poured water into a basin and began to wash His disciples' feet (John 13:1–17). They were speechless. What Jesus was doing was totally inappropriate. He was their teacher, the rabbi, the leader of this new revolution. Washing people's feet was assigned to the lowliest and least essential servant in their society, not someone like Jesus. But He knew that they were trying to position themselves for power and greatness (Luke 22:24–30). Jesus wanted to show them the true nature of Kingdom ministry.

Jesus knelt before them, washing the feet of His followers one by one. Peter tried to protest, but Jesus made it clear that this was the way of *His* kingdom and, if Peter wanted to be part, he must allow Jesus to serve him. When Jesus had finished, He put on His clothes and then asked the disciples if they understood what He had done. There was silence. Jesus then told them that to follow Him as Teacher and Lord is to do as He did. He is the Master and, as He washed their feet, they were to wash one another's feet. Jesus concluded by reminding them that followers were not greater than their Master. Service in His Kingdom would be marked by humility, not by pride.

The meal was now ready. Jesus told His disciples that He was eager to eat the Passover with them, telling the twelve that it would be the last time they would celebrate it together until the Kingdom was fulfilled (Luke 22:7–19). The Scriptures tell us that while they were eating, Jesus took bread, gave thanks, broke it, and gave it to His disciples saying, *"Take it; this is my body"* (Mark 14:22). He then took the cup and did the same thing, saying *"This is my blood of the covenant, which is poured out for many"* (Mark 14:24). And they all drank from it.

The bread and wine were symbolic of Christ's body and blood, which Jesus was soon to sacrifice on the cross for all people of all time. Today Christians everywhere celebrate the Lord's Supper and by the power of the Holy Spirit experience His resurrected presence as they participate in the sacrament. The broken bread reminds believers that their redemption was accomplished by the breaking of Christ's body at Calvary. The wine represents the blood of Jesus, reminding Christians that Jesus shed His blood on the cross as payment for their sins. Bread and wine are precious to believers, continual reminders that Jesus paid a great price to provide the gift of life to all who receive Him.

But the bread and wine Jesus gave the disciples held even more meaning for them, and for all Christians. The elements not only pointed to the sacrifice that Christ made, but they represented the true nature of Kingdom ministry. Jesus was telling His followers that ministry is all about brokenness. Just as wheat must be crushed to become bread, and grapes must be crushed to become wine, so He would be crushed and broken to bring life to people. And what was true of the master would need to be true of the servant. The disciples would soon learn that the cross would forever be the symbol of Christian ministry.

Jesus was not only showing Christians the nature of His ministry, but He was also illustrating the shape of ministry for all His followers. Christians are called to follow Christ's example, to be like Him in every way. Nowhere is this more true than in the quality and character of ministry. Responding to the sacrifice of Christ includes a willingness to surrender. That involves offering resources, and gifts, and life itself to touch the world in Jesus' name. As Jesus was broken, so Christians must be broken to serve the lost and hurting effectively. The exact shape that will take will vary person to person. But all Christians should recognize that the power of the gospel flows through the sacrifice of Christ, moving in and through the brokenness of His people. Ministry is about humility, and it is about brokenness.

An Upside-down World

Political, economic, and military power are valued by nations around the world. Global importance and standing are determined by how much of each a particular country possesses. Nations are divided between the haves and the have-nots. It is not hard to see that some nations not only have more than others, but see themselves as better because of it. More is always better in our world. And nations seem to be willing to do almost anything to get more and keep more, no matter how it might hurt another country. The fist is closed around every resource of importance and power, whether it is to grab for more or fight to keep what is already there.

This attitude is reflected in our own society, seen in the way people pursue money, position, popularity, and power. The more an individual has of any or all of these resources determines his or her standing with other people. Our culture is fascinated with celebrities, politicians, entre-preneurs, and military heroes. Television programs are exclusively dedicated to the lifestyles of the rich and famous. Magazines about glamorous and powerful people sell by the millions. There are now reality shows that promise that a special someone will become either a million-aire or celebrity, luring tens of millions to stay glued to the television screen. State lotteries boast multi-million-dollar jackpots to the lucky winner, causing people to give what they cannot afford, to win what they will never have.

This attitude of grab and greed is pervasive. It has become the focal point of advertising campaigns for countless companies which promise that their product holds the key to success and power. The desire for importance and power leads people to seek advancement, new titles, and institu-tional recognition. Life seems to be about climbing over those who are above, even if it means stepping on the backs of those who stand beneath. Being kind and fair to others is fine, as long as such attitudes do not stand in the way of progress. When they do, selfishness and manipulation become the order of the day.

The attitude of the world seems to have gained a solid foothold amongst some of God's people. Money has become quite important to many Christian leaders, so much so that they have adopted a "name it and claim it" theology that encourages believers to grab for "more." I heard one prominent televangelist remark that since the streets of heaven were lined with gold, he felt it important that God's people get used to the feel of it here. We believers also love our titles and degrees, as though they really matter in the Kingdom of God. I myself struggled with feelings of pride and accomplishment when being introduced before speaking. I enjoyed hearing my degrees, titles, publications, and positions mentioned. I felt important. How sad. How unlike Jesus.

The Church of Jesus Christ is to operate by a completely different set of principles. It is, in fact, an upside-down Kingdom. The bottom is the top, less is more, and giving is more important than receiving. The only title that means anything is "child of God," the highest position is kneeling on the floor, and the least get the most. Others, whoever they may be, are most important, the only robe that matters is that of Christ's righteousness, and the capital of the Kingdom is love, not money, which can only be kept by giving it away. In God's Kingdom victory comes to those who surrender, freedom to those captive to Christ, and strength to people who admit they are weak. And most importantly, ministry involves a willingness to be broken so that others can become whole. This was the way of Jesus. It must also be the shape of ministry for all who seek to become like Him in life.

Jesus, the Wounded Healer

Many people of Jesus' day did not accept Him as the promised Messiah because He did not fit the profile of the deliverer that had evolved over the centuries. The Israelites had been waiting for a Messiah that would free them from Roman oppression. They were expecting Him to lead a geopolitical revolt and reestablish a golden age of Davidic reign over the nation. Even Jesus' closest disciples entertained such notions. They were convinced that the Messiah would establish an earthly Kingdom, with mighty armies blessed by God. They expected the Messiah to be a person of incredible power and influence in the affairs of the Jewish nation. Jesus was none of those. And when in the final days of His life people saw that, they stopped following and started to shout for His death.

The ministry of Jesus Christ was centered upon Kingdom power, not political, economic, or military might. And His ministry style was based upon a servant–leader model, as opposed to one of worldly authority and prestige. He never intended to sit upon the throne in Jerusalem. He was more concerned to establish God's reign over the hearts of lost and broken people. Jesus wanted to set people free from the oppression of dark spiritual forces. He had an eternal perspective and wanted to make a way for all people to live in abundance for all eternity, not just free one nation for a mere lifespan.

Hundreds of years before Jesus came, the prophet Isaiah spoke of a servant who would come to serve the people of Israel. It is incredible to read his words and see how they accurately point to the sacrificial ministry of Jesus Christ. I encourage you to ask the Holy Spirit to open your eyes and hearts as you read this wonderful passage about the Suffering Servant:

> *"See, my servant will act wisely;*
> *he will be raised and lifted up and highly*
> *exalted.*

Just as there were many who were appalled at him –
his appearance was so disfigured beyond that of any man
and his form marred beyond human likeness –
so will he sprinkle many nations,
and kings will shut their mouths because of him.
For what they were not told, they will see,
and what they have not heard, they will understand.

Who has believed our message
and to whom has the arm of the Lord *been revealed?*
He grew up before him like a tender shoot,
and like a root out of dry ground.
He had no beauty or majesty to attract us to him,
nothing in his appearance that we should desire him.
He was despised and rejected by men,
a man of sorrows, and familiar with suffering.
Like one from whom men hide their faces
he was despised, and we esteemed him not.

Surely he took up our infirmities
and carried our sorrows,
yet we considered him stricken by God,
smitten by him, and afflicted.
But he was pierced for our transgressions,
he was crushed for our iniquities;
the punishment that brought us peace was upon him,
and by his wounds we are healed.
We all, like sheep, have gone astray,
each of us has turned to his own way;
and the Lord *has laid on him*
the iniquity of us all.

He was oppressed and afflicted,
yet he did not open his mouth;

he was led like a lamb to the slaughter,
and as a sheep before her shearers is silent,
so he did not open his mouth.
By oppression and judgment he was taken away.
And who can speak of his descendants?
For he was cut off from the land of the living;
for the transgression of my people he was stricken.
He was assigned a grave with the wicked,
and with the rich in his death,
though he had done no violence,
nor was any deceit in his mouth.

Yet it was the LORD*'s will to crush him and cause him to*
suffer,
and though the LORD *makes his life a guilt offering,*
he will see his offspring and prolong his days,
and the will of the LORD *will prosper in his hand.*
After the suffering of his soul,
he will see the light of life and be satisfied;
by his knowledge my righteous servant will justify many,
and he will bear their iniquities.
Therefore I will give him a portion among the great,
and he will divide the spoils with the strong,
because he poured out his life unto death,
and was numbered with the transgressors.
For he bore the sin of many,
and made intercession for the transgressors.''

(Isaiah 52:13–53:12)

This wonderful prophecy is speaking about Jesus and His sacrificial ministry to all people. Jesus did not come to be served, to gain great power, or to rule on an earthly throne. Jesus came to serve the broken and lost, and gave His life to give them eternal life. As this text prophesied, Jesus had a ministry of suffering. He bore our infirmities, carried our sorrows, and was crushed and cut off from God. Jesus gave when others would have taken, was silent when others would have shouted, and willingly surrendered His life when many would have fought to stay alive. He was punished though He had done no wrong, and was violently treated though He had done no violence.

Wounds that Heal

Isaiah said that the suffering servant would bring healing to people through His many wounds. That is clearly a reference to the heart of Christ's ministry. He was a wounded healer, as Father Henri Nouwen suggested in his magnificent book of the same title. The power of God actually flows into our lives as it passes through the wounds of Christ. We find healing for our bodies, minds, spirits, and relationships through the broken places in Christ's body. This is the ultimate contrast between the kingdoms of this world and the Kingdom of God. Healing is only possible because Jesus, the Son of God, was brutally wounded by the people He came to heal.

The wounds of Christ are precious to Christians. They not only represent the sacrifice that Jesus made for our redemption, they actually provide healing to the broken. That is why the cross, which was for many a sign of shame, is to Christians the most cherished symbol of the faith. The cross is the centerpiece of Christian belief, the place where Jesus paid for our sin, received our punishment, and set us free from the forces of evil darkness. Where others see defeat, we see victory, and where others see death, Christians see life, all made possible because of the sacrificial nature of Christ's life and ministry.

Jesus made it very clear to His followers that they too must embrace a ministry of sacrifice and brokenness. He told the disciples that they must be willing to be persecuted, misunderstood, and rejected by people as they served the Kingdom of God. He let them know that there would be a price to pay, including the call to carry a cross as He did. While He promised them power, it would be spiritual power, not political, and it was only to be used to set others free. Jesus made it clear that ministry was about helping the broken and lost, not about gaining importance or position. There was no promise of great fame, or wealth, or exalted position. Jesus told the disciples that ministry was serious business that would cost them everything. But He promised to be with them always, and one day welcome them into a place of eternal joy.

It is clear from Scripture and the testimony of history that the disciples understood the nature of Christian ministry. They did not seek titles, amass great wealth, or wield incredible political power. The disciples were servants, who sought to touch the broken in Jesus' name. They preached the message of the cross, were persecuted, beaten, rejected, and imprisoned for their faith. The disciples fed the hungry, healed the sick, and set people free from demonic oppression. In the end, most died horrible deaths as Christian martyrs. Why? Because they were followers of Jesus Christ and their ministries reflected His ministry.

These early Christian disciples were not perfect. They had their problems, weaknesses, and failings. There were arguments, misunderstandings and more than a few mistakes. But they loved Jesus and responded to the call to be broken for the world. That was the true shape of Christian ministry for them. Like Jesus, they allowed their own wounds to become a source of healing to others. Where Jesus touched them, they in turn touched others. They received in order to give.

Paul spoke of this "blessed to be a blessing" concept in 2 Corinthians. He said that God comforts His children when they are in trouble, so that they can in turn comfort other people when they are having a difficult time (2 Corinthians 1:3–7). In other words Christ's wounds bring healing to my wounds which, if I allow, flows over to bring healing to others as well. I have actually seen this at work in my own life in a most unexpected way.

I did not receive an instantaneous healing from depression and agoraphobia. In fact, I wrestled for months with the depression, and spent over a decade suffering through severe anxiety. As difficult as these days were, two amazing things have taken place in my life as a result. First, the Lord has met me in the most amazing ways. He has entered my life to bring strength during very tough times, and actually healed several deep emotional wounds that were crippling me in life. And the trial has actually drawn me much closer to the Lord. Second, Jesus has given me an unexpected ministry to emotionally broken people.

For almost ten years now I have been blessed of Jesus to pray with hundreds of people who were locked in deep bondage because of emotional wounds. I would have never dreamed about being used in this way. I went to seminary and even received a doctorate with the intention of being a super-pastor who could build great churches. But Jesus wanted my ministry to align with His, and so He allowed suffering to shape a new calling in my life. The Lord has even allowed me to write several books that help people understand deep wounding and receive the healing touch of the Lord. I, a person who is still in the process of being healed by Jesus, have been used by the Lord as a vessel of healing to others. What an amazing upside-down Kingdom this is!

I earlier admitted that I experienced great personal pride

as I was introduced before speaking. It was as if all my accomplishments somehow qualified me to serve others. That has radically changed. Now I am often introduced as a person who was institutionalized for depression and anxiety, yet met Jesus in a brand new way. Amazingly, I find people far more anxious to hear what I have to say than they did before. It is because they know I was wounded, just like many of them. And they want to know how Jesus touched me, in the hope that He would do the same for them, which He usually does. The comfort I have received is overflowing, all to the glory of Jesus Christ. By His mercy Jesus has moved me into a place of true ministry, one that flows through my own brokenness. Out of my weakness has come an incredible sense of the Lord's power, and lives are being changed (2 Corinthians 12:9).

Nourishment and Nurture

You are part of a movement that is unlike any other on the face of the earth. You are called to become a wounded healer of Jesus Christ. You are asked by Jesus to offer your brokenness to Him as a channel of healing power to those who are lost and hurting in the world. He does not want you to pretend to be all together so that you can fool people into believing that you are qualified to speak for Him. Jesus wants you to invite Him to touch the battered parts of your life, and from the comfort you receive turn and do the same for other struggling people. He has clearly shown you that ministry is about serving others, about humility, about brokenness. Jesus calls you to be like Him, willingly carrying a cross so that others can be forever free.

The seed of Christ's nature dwells within you. That means that you have the potential to be a wounded healer of Jesus Christ. While the concept is contrary to the way of the world, it is not contrary to who you are as a child of God. The Holy Spirit is positioned to help you grow into the likeness of Christ, which means that His ministry truly can become your ministry. It will take the Spirit's power to nourish and nurture that potential. I want to suggest five specific ways that you can help that process.

First, read Scripture, particularly the Gospels, in order to get a clear understanding of the ministry of Jesus. Ask the Holy Spirit to help you see the sacrificial nature of His ministry to lost and hurting people. Spend time reading John 13, where Jesus serves His disciples and celebrates the Last Supper. Read about the arrest of Jesus, the cruel treatment He had at the hands of the soldiers, and the mocking that He endured. Meditate on the scourging, as Jesus received thirty-nine stripes, wounds that now provide healing to the broken. Of course, read about the crucifixion, when Jesus was nailed to a cross as the once-and-for-all sacrifice for sin. Slowly pray through Isaiah's prophecy about the suffering servant. These texts will forever seal in your heart the truth that Christ's ministry was all about brokenness. You will see that we are called to be like Him, a cross-carrying people who are broken and blessed and given that others may be whole.

Second, ask the Holy Spirit to search your heart for any ways in which you have embraced the world's concept of leadership. Power, money, and position can be very seductive. If you are not careful they can get a foothold in your life. They certainly did with the Pharisees. Many Christians today have rationalized that such things are important, even vital to life. The power of this deception is great, and so we must be ever watchful. I know that I must keep these issues before the Lord in prayer at all times. Our society is permeated with the concept that being on top is the only place to live, and that the rod and scepter are necessary to success. Jesus tells us different, calling you and me to kneel to serve and carry a towel, and a basin.

Third, you would do well to allow Jesus to touch your own deep wounds. This was addressed at length in the previous chapter. Our dear Lord cares deeply about the emotional abuse and disappointment that you have experienced in life. He desires to touch you tenderly, promising to have compassion upon you in the place of your pain (Isaiah 49:13). His wounds hold healing for you and the hope of freedom and new life. Jesus came to minister to your deep needs and was willingly afflicted so that you can be whole. Remember that Jesus was broken for you, even in those hidden areas that you try so hard to forget. Allow His healing light into those dark places, and experience His love in ways you never knew possible.

Fourth, allow the broken places to become a source of healing to others. Most people in ministry attempt to serve Christ from their strengths, keeping hidden the deepest weaknesses, wounds, and failures of their lives. Usually there is a great deal of pain and shame attached to such things, so they are locked away where no one will ever see. In many ways that is a strategy of the evil one to keep people in bondage.

I have learned, through the grace of Jesus Christ, that where I am weak He is strong. My failures have often been the context of the Lord's greatest ministry to my life. These wounds have, when touched of Christ, become a source of incredible healing to others. I well remember being told never to admit that I was in a psychiatric hospital. I was warned that my ministry would end if I ever let that fact be known. But Jesus met me behind those locked doors and I simply had to take the risk and tell. I am so glad the Holy Spirit gave me the strength to do that. It has unlocked more doors for ministry than I ever would have imagined. What

He did for me He will do for you. Allow the comfort that you receive from Christ to flow through to other hurting people. Become a true wounded healer.

Fifth, I encourage you to read authors who believe that ministry flows from brokenness. Larry Crabb, Joni Erickson-Tada, Henri Nouwen, and Charles Colson have each impacted my own understanding of the true nature of Christian ministry. They each tell of meeting the Lord in very difficult times, and then seeing Jesus touch others through their lives. What they once saw as their shame and weakness has become a source of healing to tens of thousands. They follow a long tradition of wounded healers who were not ashamed to admit that Jesus met them in some pretty dark places. Their names have been added to a list that includes people like Peter, James and John, Paul, and Mary Magdalene. There were also people like Simon the Leper, the Gadarene demoniac, Blind Bartimaus, and a nameless person only remembered as the woman who was caught in adultery. These precious men and women have been remembered, not because they were so good and strong, but because Jesus touched them with healing power and set them free.

You are invited to move toward spiritual maturity and become like Jesus. It is an awesome calling that is beyond all human strength and possibility. But the seed of Jesus is alive within you. That is a promise from God and a hope that can be increasingly realized through the power of the Holy Spirit. You can become a wounded healer who ministers life to a healing world. It all begins by bowing before the Lord, and humbly saying yes.

Chapter 8

Empowerment

When I entered Geneva College as a freshman I was befriended by an older student named Paul. He was one of the most interesting people I had ever met. Paul was bright, intelligent, sensitive, and socially aware. He deeply cared about people, spent time with the ostracized and downcast, and spoke out about pressing social issues of the day. He protested American involvement in Vietnam, was serious about social reform, and appropriately challenged existing structures of authority. Paul did all this with respect, but also with conviction and determination. I learned important lessons from Paul about what was right and important in life.

Paul was also great fun and could be thoroughly out-rageous. I remember that while all of us were growing beards, he grew what he called "spots." Paul would shave his face, except for two round spots, which he let grow until they looked like horns protruding from his chin. He also could be hilarious at an athletic event. If a player would mess up most fans would yell something like, "You stink. Go home!" Not Paul. He would shout out to the player, "It's okay, I'm sure you're good at other things!" Or he would comment loudly about how nice the player looked in his uniform, all of which was far more humiliating. Once, the administration made it clear that students were no longer permitted to go barefooted to class. Paul took a pair of gym shoes, cut the bottoms out, and proceeded to go through registration in full view of teachers and administration. I thought it one of the funniest things I had ever seen. But not everyone shared my opinion.

People could get very uptight about Paul. While they appreciated his gifts, some would have preferred that he be less outrageous. At times his actions embarrassed certain people. Administrators tried to talk with Paul, asking him if possible to calm down a bit and rethink some of what he was doing. Paul could make people uncomfortable, and they always concluded that the problem was surely with him, not them. He was wonderfully unpredictable, which made many people very nervous. They would have liked it if Paul were less visible as a representative of the Geneva College student body.

I share this story about Paul because I believe it can serve as a metaphor for the attitude many people have about the person of the Holy Spirit. There is no doubt but that the Holy Spirit is loving, caring, and deeply committed to God's people. He often ministers in very gentle ways to people, moving in and through lives like a warm, refreshing summer breeze. The Holy Spirit is spoken of in Scripture as the Comforter, Spirit of Truth, Counselor, and Wind of God. The Bible says that the Holy Spirit will help Christians through life, teach them about Jesus, guide them into truth, and help them discern the difference between what is of God and what is of the evil one. Jesus promised that the Holy Spirit would always be with Christians, strengthening them to resist temptation and walk in holiness. Christians like these truths about the Holy Spirit and welcome Him into their lives and churches to minister all these promises.

But there is another side to the Holy Spirit, one that makes many people very uncomfortable. He can be quite unpredictable and outrageous at times. Take Pentecost, for example. There was nothing gentle about the way He came rushing into the upper room, lighting the disciples aflame and sending them out into the streets babbling like drunkards. He was hardly behaving like a comforter that day. He certainly was not going unnoticed. In fact, much of the Holy Spirit's ministry that is recorded in the New Testament is like that. He would move in great power, shaking up people's lives, rattling buildings, bringing the dead to life, and causing some of the living to fall dead. The Holy Spirit took Philip on a wild ride out of Gaza, knocked Saul senseless, healed people through shadows and prayer cloths, and anointed everyday people with incredible supernatural gifts of power.

There is no doubt that many Christians are so uncomfortable, even embarrassed, by this side of the Holy Spirit that they have marginalized much of His ministry in the local church. Some have tried to argue that He does not work such signs and wonders today, though the evidence of history clearly says otherwise. Many leaders have put restrictions on what can happen within their churches, trying to tame the Spirit's ministry and domesticate Him. All it really does is quench the fire of His presence and turn Christianity into a powerless religion based on empty rituals and human effort.

Demonstrations of Power

In his first letter to the church in Corinth Paul stated that he did not come to them with wise and persuasive words. Instead, he came preaching Christ with a demonstration of the Holy Spirit's power (1 Corinthians 2:1–4). Paul was saying that words are not enough. People need to see and sense the power of God that is manifested through the ministry of the Holy Spirit. How different from my experience, particularly in seminary. For three years I barely heard mention of the Holy Spirit. Seminary was about words and wisdom, not ministering in the power of the Holy Spirit. The underlying assumption was that if I had enough knowledge I could be effective in leading a local congregation to spiritual maturity. Hundreds, possibly thousands, of men and women were educated in seminaries that held this view.

The result seems obvious to me. Too many local churches have become places where words are the main focus of ministry, not power. Many Christian leaders talk about renewal, even adopting programs that promise to bring new life to struggling congregations. But, once again, the ministry of the Holy Spirit is marginalized for fear that "things will get out of control." I am not arguing that there should not be discernment and caution when it comes to power ministry. Leaders need to be watchful, following the admonition in 1 Thessalonians 5:21 to test everything. But many have so feared the misuse of spiritual power that they have opted for disuse, which is clearly contrary to the command of Scripture (1 Thessalonians 5:19–22). Recently a colleague stated that his congregation does not test things, because there is frankly nothing to test. Everything is safe and in order, and absent of power.

The impact that this is having upon individual Christians is tragic. Instead of being equipped to mature in the Holy Spirit, they are struggling to respond to the call of Christ in their own strength. The sense of wonder regarding the supernatural nature of following Jesus is seriously diminished. There is also an obvious chasm between the testimony of Scripture and the experience that they are having as followers of Jesus Christ. This weakens not only the individual Christian, but the witness of the church to an unbelieving world.

I am convinced that if the Apostle Paul returned to comment on the ministry of the local church he would, in far too many places, wonder what happened. The presence of the Holy Spirit, moving through ordinary people who use their spiritual gifts, was to be normative in local congregations. Such signs and wonders were evidences that the Kingdom of God was truly present. Paul told the Corinthians that the Kingdom of God was not a matter of talk. It was a matter of power, Holy Spirit power (1 Corinthians 4:20). The absence of power in local churches is a cause of much decline being experienced within denominations today. Many people find church boring and irrelevant and are leaving in search of something more.

The movement of the Holy Spirit in the last century has opened many people's eyes to the power of God that is available. Pentecostalism, the Charismatic movement, and the more recent outpourings of the Holy Spirit have attracted tens of millions of followers worldwide. People are discovering that God still moves today, filling everyday believers with the power of the Holy Spirit. Many believers are ministering spiritual gifts that include prophecy, healing, deliverance, and intercessory prayer. Granted, there can be some abuse and immaturity in these movements. That is, of course, no more or less true than in those churches that are closed to the working of the Holy Spirit. But time and sound teaching have enabled many people to grow and become a mighty force for God on earth.

The ministry of the Holy Spirit is essential to vital Christian living. People cannot grow to experience spiritual maturity without being open to His presence and power. They will never become like Jesus, because only the Holy Spirit holds the power that transforms people into His likeness. Human effort will only lead to frustration and failure. Christians must open their lives to the Spirit's touch. Admittedly there will be some fear, for the Holy Spirit is not tame. But He is good and only does what is necessary to enliven believers as representatives of the Kingdom of God.

Most people that I know want to take the risk. They know that only the Holy Spirit will change and empower them to minister in Jesus' name. Initially there may be some apprehension. But I know that many believers, including me, are hungry for more of God in their lives. Once they experience the power of the Holy Spirit they will never turn back to powerless Christianity.

Jesus and the Ministry of the Holy Spirit

Every aspect of Christ's life and ministry was intricately related to the person of the Holy Spirit. If we are to become like Him, that must be true of us as well. Jesus' life on earth began when the Holy Spirit hovered over Mary at the conception (Luke 1:35). After His birth, it was the Holy Spirit that anointed Simeon in the temple court as He held Jesus in His arms and gave praise to God for bringing the Messiah to Israel (Luke 2:25–32). When Jesus came out of the waters of the Jordan at His baptism, the Holy Spirit descended upon Him in the form of a dove, anointing Him to begin His earthly ministry (Luke 3:22). The Holy Spirit then led Jesus into the desert, where for forty days He was tempted by the devil (Luke 4:1).

Jesus went into the synagogue in Nazareth and stood to read. He was handed the scroll of the prophet Isaiah and Jesus turned to the following passage:

"The Spirit of the Lord is on me,
  because he has anointed me
  to preach good news to the poor.
He has sent me to proclaim freedom for the prisoners
  and recovery of sight for the blind,
to release the oppressed,
  to proclaim the year of the Lord's favor."

                    (Isaiah 61:1–2, quoted in Luke 4:18–19)

Jesus sat down and every eye was fixed upon Him. He then told them that the scripture had been fulfilled in their hearing that day (Luke 4:14–21). Jesus was the anointed servant that Isaiah had prophesied, filled with the power of the Holy Spirit to preach, heal, and deliver those who were locked in darkness.

From that day forward Jesus ministered in the power of the Holy Spirit. His teaching had a depth of wisdom that was unparalleled among Jewish religious leaders. Jesus preached the Kingdom of God in the power of the Holy Spirit, drawing great crowds who amassed to hear His good news. The Holy Spirit empowered Jesus to heal the sick, and the Gospels include many accounts of the blind seeing, the deaf hearing, the paralyzed walking, the leprous being cleansed, and the dead being brought back to life.

Even the religious leaders of His day recognized that Jesus was a miracle worker, but attributed His power to the influence of the evil one. They accused Christ of casting out demons by the power of darkness. Jesus said that He drove out demons by the power of the Holy Spirit. He then warned them that God would forgive many sins, but those committed against the Holy Spirit would not be forgiven, ever (Matthew 12:22–37). Jesus honored the presence of the Holy Spirit, knowing that the Spirit's presence was essential to His life and ministry on earth.

One of the very first statements made about Jesus was that He came to baptize people in the power of the Holy Spirit (Mark 1:8). Jesus intended that His followers would have the same relationship with the Holy Spirit that He did. He never gave any impression that the power He had for ministry was exclusive to Him. On the contrary, Jesus told His followers that they not only could but must have the Holy Spirit in their lives. When Nicodemus came to talk with Jesus about the Kingdom of God, Jesus told him that he had to be born again. At first Nicodemus was confused as to what Jesus was saying. Jesus explained that membership in the Kingdom of God required that a person was born of the Holy Spirit. He went on to say that this new birth was the very reason that Jesus was sent from God, so that people could have eternal life as God's gift (John 3:1–21).

While the term "born again" has lost favor in some circles, it is an essential part of the Christian experience. Men, women, and children who receive Jesus are indwelt by the Holy Spirit. The same Holy Spirit who empowered Jesus Christ establishes residence deep inside believers. The transaction that takes place is an act of God's grace that gives people an eternal place in the household of God. It is profound, personal, and in many ways defies description. When I was born again of the Holy Spirit I felt as though I came alive for the very first time. Those who have experienced that new birth know exactly what I mean. It is supernatural.

Jesus once declared that those who believed in Him would have streams of living water flowing from their inner being (John 7:37–39). John writes that Jesus was referring to the presence of the Holy Spirit that was to be poured out upon believers. How wonderful that image is. A stream is a constant source of life, power, and refreshment, and Jesus said that the Holy Spirit would be like that for believers. His presence would be an incredible resource for victorious personal living as God's chosen children.

How desperately I need the Source of Life, but must confess that for many years I did not seriously consider the presence of the Holy Spirit in my ministry. Many times I stood to preach, barely ministering a drop of real Kingdom power. All the while a living stream of His presence was available within me. When I finally opened myself to the Spirit's presence, I experienced a new level of anointing and intimacy. Nothing has been the same since. And the promise of Jesus regarding streams of the Holy Spirit is as true for you as it is for me.

Jesus spent a considerable amount of time teaching His disciples about the ministry of the Holy Spirit. That was especially true as He neared the cross. On the night of His betrayal, Jesus promised the disciples that He would send the Holy Spirit to them upon His return to heaven. He called the Spirit the "Paraclete," which can mean counselor and comforter (John 14:16). Jesus told His followers that the Holy Spirit would stand with them in life, helping them fulfill the ministry that Jesus was leaving in their hands. Jesus called the Holy Spirit "the Spirit of truth," and promised the disciples that He would teach them new truths, as well as remind them of what Jesus had said to them (John 14:25; 15:26). Jesus told them that it was actually good that He was going away because His departure would make room for the coming of the Holy Spirit (John 16:7).

Following the resurrection Jesus met with His disciples and twice reminded them of the importance of the Holy Spirit's ministry. Once He came into their presence and breathed on them, saying, *"Receive the Holy Spirit"* (John 20:22). Then at the ascension, He gave them specific instructions to gather in Jerusalem and wait for the Spirit's arrival. He told them that they would each be baptized with the

Holy Spirit, which Jesus saw as essential to their great commission. He told the disciples that the Holy Spirit would give them power and they in turn would be His witnesses to the ends of the earth (Acts 1:4–8).

The disciples did as Jesus instructed and the promised Holy Spirit did come. Fifty days after the resurrection the Breath of God blew upon them as they gathered together in prayer. Flames of fire appeared upon their heads and they spilled out into the street speaking in tongues. The people were amazed as they heard the gospel in their own languages. Three thousand people gave their hearts to Christ that day, and the Church was born (Acts 2:1–41).

The disciples were never the same again. They went forward in the power of the Holy Spirit to preach the gospel, heal the sick, and deliver people from demonic bondage. The Church grew from a handful of followers to a fast-growing movement that numbered in the tens of thousands. The Holy Spirit empowered ordinary men and women to take the message of Christ into the regions beyond Jerusalem. They worked signs and wonders through the Spirit that convinced people that Jesus was the Son of God and that the Kingdom of God was breaking into the world. Like Jesus, these early followers of Christ were people of the Holy Spirit. Christians today cannot afford to be anything less.

The Holy Spirit in the Writings of Paul

Was the movement of the Holy Spirit restricted to the original disciples? Or did the Lord intend for all believers to be empowered by His presence? Were demonstrations of His power limited to the first few years after the resurrection of Christ? Or should Christians today still expect to minister as the early disciples did? I believe the answer to those questions can be found in the writings of the Apostle Paul.

Recognized as the Church's greatest theologian, Paul wrote in order to help believers understand the nature and function of the Church of Jesus Christ. His epistles are recognized as the inspired word of God and as such instructive to all Christians. That means that we can personalize his teachings into our own lives and ministries.

Paul makes it clear that all Christians receive the Holy Spirit at conversion and that His presence in our lives is a down payment of our future inheritance (Ephesians 1:13–14). This promise is not reserved for spiritual superstars. It is for every child of God. Paul taught that the presence of the Spirit is evidence that a person truly belongs to the Lord. Paul encouraged his readers to rely on the Spirit in every possible way, for His primary ministry was to help us in our weaknesses (Romans 8).

According to Paul, the Holy Spirit has given every Christian spiritual gifts to be used within the body of Christ. These gifts are listed in three main scriptures: Romans 12, 1 Corinthians 12, and Ephesians 4. The apostle Paul said that Christians would manifest these gifts in different ways and with varying degrees of power (1 Corinthians 12:4–6). But he was adamant that every believer is supernaturally empowered to minister spiritual gifts.

These truths should excite believers and motivate them to discover more and more about the ministry of the Holy Spirit in their lives. The Spirit that brought Jesus back from the dead is alive within the people of God. He has provided supernatural gifts of grace that can be discovered, developed, and used by Christians. These giftings are channels of Kingdom power that can literally transform lives. Believers are admonished to allow the Holy Spirit to fill them to overflowing so that His presence and power flows like streams of living water.

Christians must take seriously the call to *"be filled with the*

Spirit." Paul penned those words under the anointing of the Holy Spirit as he was writing to the Christians in Ephesus (Ephesians 5:18). Christians must recognize several key points about these words. First, they are stated in the imperative, which means they are a command. This infilling is not an option that believers can lightly consider. It is a command that must be obeyed by all people who intend to follow the Lord faithfully.

The words *"be filled with the Spirit"* are also generally delivered, which means that they are for everyone. The verb form used in the Greek also signifies that this infilling is to be a repeated event. Christians are commanded to be filled over and over again. The implication is that being filled with the Holy Spirit is an experience that happens regularly in a Christian's life, overflowing through them to the people they serve. This repeated experience of empowerment is meant to be normative for all who minister in Jesus' name. Unquestionably then it is meant for you and for me.

Nourishment and Nurture

Jesus walked this earth in the power of the Holy Spirit. As you are well aware by now, the call of Christ is that you would be like Him. The good news is that the Holy Spirit is already present within your spirit, ever since the day you surrendered your life to Christ. You are not missing some essential ingredient to being a spiritually mature follower of Christ. Right now, even as you read these words, the Holy Spirit, who hovered over creation, anointed Moses and David, descended upon Christ, raised Him from the dead, and enflamed the disciples at Pentecost, dwells in you! There is a stream of living water ready to break forth in your life, bringing power and refreshment to you and Kingdom ministry to others. All you need is to allow the Holy Spirit to nourish and nurture the treasure that is already in your life. I want to suggest several ways that can happen.

First, take Jesus at His word. Ask the Holy Spirit to guide you into all truth. Jesus said that He would be your counselor, teaching you deep things about the Kingdom. Ask the Spirit to fulfill Christ's promise. Spend some time in prayer and actually talk to the Holy Spirit. Tell Him that you know that He is present and willing to lead you into spiritual maturity. That is why Jesus has given Him to you. Do not be afraid that somehow you will lose focus on the centrality of Christ. Jesus assured His followers that the Holy Spirit always brings glory to Him. The Holy Spirit keeps Jesus in the light whenever He ignites people with His presence and power.

Second, read scriptures that focus upon the person and work of the Holy Spirit. I encourage you to read the Gospels, particularly John. The Holy Spirit is repeatedly mentioned by Jesus in John's Gospel, with specific instructions regarding His ministry to Christians. The book of Acts is the story of the Holy Spirit's coming at Pentecost and His dynamic ministry through first-century believers. It is one of the most exciting stories in all Scripture, chronicling the growth of the Church through the power of the Holy Spirit. There are accounts of dramatic encounters with God in the book of Acts that highlight the Spirit's ministry. And of course read the epistles of Paul. Romans 8 and 1 Corinthians 12–14 are especially important. The Holy Spirit will teach you through this study and birth an even greater hunger in your life for His presence and power.

Third, prayerfully read books that have been written by people who have experienced the deeper life of the Holy Spirit. I have been challenged and inspired by reading such literature. There are many important titles, but I have been profoundly impacted by the following:

- *Christianity with Power* by Charles Kraft
- *God's Empowering Presence* by Gordon Fee
- *Into the Depths with God* by Calvin Miller
- *Surprised by the Power of the Holy Spirit* by Jack Deere
- *The Comforter* by A.W. Tozer
- *The Gentle Ministry of the Holy Spirit* by A.B. Simpson
- *The Holy Spirit* by Billy Graham
- *The Third Wave of the Holy Spirit* by Peter Wagner

While these books represent a variety of theological tradi-tions, they each affirm the critical ministry that the Holy Spirit has in the lives of Christ's followers. You will find that the Spirit will stir your heart as you read, quickening a hunger to go deeper with Him.

Fourth, pray and ask the Holy Spirit to anoint you with His presence. John the Baptist said that God gives the Spirit without limit (John 3:35). Jesus said that the Father would faithfully give the Spirit to all who ask (Luke 11:13). These scriptures should encourage you to seek openly the infilling that the word of God promises. I encourage you not to seek any particular manifestation. The experience of His touch varies from person to person. The key is to ask in faith, believing that this is a prayer that the Spirit loves to answer. I clearly remember when that prayer began to take shape in my own life. The hunger for more of His presence began to grow until I could hardly bear the intensity of the desire. Then in a moment, He was there like never before, and everything changed forever. God will answer that prayer, I assure you.

Fifth, consider finding a gathering of God's people who are open to the movement of the Holy Spirit and attend several of their meetings. This might mean going to a prayer meeting, or Bible study, or even a special seminar or conference on the Holy Spirit. Take time before going to find out if they are balanced and mature believers who keep Jesus central and honor the Word of God. If they do, take the risk and check things out. Feel free just to wait and watch. That is what I did when I first became exposed to the ministry of the Holy Spirit. Admittedly there was at first more than a bit of nervousness. But soon I saw that the people who genuinely moved in the Holy Spirit loved Jesus and cared deeply for each other. Their life in the Spirit soon ignited my own life, and a transformation took place that has in many ways never stopped.

The Holy Spirit is alive and well and moving powerfully across the earth today. His ministry is as dynamic and transforming as it was in the first century. Sadly, not everyone is aware or open to His presence and power. Where and when that is true, Christianity is powerless and essentially ineffective. But when people begin to open to His ministry exciting things begin to happen. That was true in the lives of Jesus and the disciples, and can be just as true in your life.

The call of Christ is an invitation to become like Him. The seed of that potential is already present within you, waiting for the transforming touch of the Holy Spirit. Allow Him to empower your life. Let Him fill you with His presence. I assure you that He is more than willing. He is waiting for you to ask, and when you do so, be ready for life to change in the most wonderful and exciting ways. You will be more like Jesus.

Chapter 9

Authority

My childhood was spent in a growing suburban neighborhood in post Second World War America. There were kids everywhere, living proof that the baby boom was a genuine sociological reality. I was an active part of a band of rambunctious boys who were close in age and interest. We spent hours together after school and during summer breaks playing in the wooded lots around our homes. One of our very favorite pastimes was playing army. We would construct bunkers, dig foxholes, and set up small logs as artillery. We would gather apples, which served as hand grenades, and set out through the trees to fight our imagined enemy, which in our case happened always to be Nazis.

Virtually all our fathers had served in the military during the war. That meant that uniforms, medals, and accessories were in good supply. We would each arrive to play wearing greatly oversized shirts that our dads had brought home from their years in the service. Some were from the Marines, Navy, and Army Air Corps. But most were from the infantry, olive drab combat fatigues that were well worn and faded. Of course, most important of all were the stripes on the sleeve. Even as children, we knew that the number of stripes determined who was in charge or, as we put it, who was boss.

Luckily for me, most of the boys wore shirts with the rank of private or corporal. Mine was a sergeant's shirt with three stripes. That gave me the right to boss everyone else around on the pretend battlefield. Oh, there were plenty of arguments and scuffles. Someone was usually threatening to quit and go home if they didn't get their way. But in the end I barked out the orders of the day, determining who went where and who had to play dead during the battle. It was great fun and I really felt like I had power. That is until the new kid moved into the neighborhood.

Mike arrived to play one day at the invitation of one of the regular boys, and everything changed. His dad had been a second lieutenant in the army and Mike was wearing a shirt with a yellow bar on the shoulder. We all knew that officers were the real bosses, and so I had to become just another soldier following orders, a humbling transition that took me a little while to accept. But in spite of all my yelling and arguing, I knew that those with more authority called the shots. We had all learned that from our dads, who had experienced the seriousness of obeying commands when, tragically, war was not a game. Authority to them had been a matter of life and death. Frankly, authority is still an important issue in life, especially when it comes to spiritual issues.

Satan, God, and Spiritual Authority

Jesus was sent from heaven with a clear mission. He came to defeat the evil one and set people free from his control. Jesus arrived with the full authority of the heavenly Father behind Him. While Satan is a powerful spirit being, he was never a match for God. His power and influence do have limits. From before the foundations of the earth God was, and is, sovereign. He holds limitless power, beyond our ability even to comprehend.

All of creation, including angels and all other spirit beings exist under God and must submit to His commands. Since the Fall Satan and his demons had free reign on earth, using their limited power to destroy God's creation. But in the fullness of time Jesus arrived. God had promised redemption and Jesus came to fulfill His word. He was given the power and authority necessary to bring down Satan and his followers.

When Jesus came the entire earth was occupied territory. The evil one and his dark minions were wreaking havoc in people's lives all across the globe. They were hell bent on destroying everything that was right and good, working to imprison men, women, and children in eternal darkness. The battle was spiritual, but it affected every aspect of life on earth. People were in bondage to all types of sin, oppressed by demonic powers, and afflicted with disorders and diseases that held them in the cruelest of captivity. Worst of all, people were separated from God, eternally lost and alone. They were living a long way from Eden and life was not good.

The Scriptures are very clear about the influence demonic beings have in the world. The Apostle Paul said that the real battles people face are against spiritual principalities and powers. That is why he encouraged believers to be strong in the Lord and the strength of His might (Ephesians 6:10–12). The New Testament explicitly teaches that demonic spirits are evil (Luke 11:24–26), intend to do harm to people (Mark 9:17–18), work to deceive people (1 Timothy 4:1), can be the cause of sickness and death (Mark 5:2–4), and brutally torment people (Mark 5:1–18).

The people of Jesus' day did not question the reality of spiritual beings. They had experienced the torment and darkness of evil spirits and were living as virtual prisoners of war. Life was very difficult for them, with many people living in varying degrees of bondage and affliction. Violence, greed, and selfishness were common, a result of an evil presence that brought great oppression and heartache to countless people. In every sense of the word people were lost, enslaved in sin, and eternally separated from God. It would take a great power to liberate these people from the death grip of Satan, an authority that they had no choice but to obey. That is precisely why God sent Jesus to earth.

Amazed at Christ's Authority

The people of Christ's day were amazed by His authority. It was obvious to them that He was not like other religious leaders. When Jesus spoke, something happened deep inside the listeners. His words carried a power that seemed supernatural to them. He also worked signs and wonders that convinced many that He was sent from God. People were healed, the dead were raised to life, and demons were subject to His commands. Even those who opposed Him saw that Jesus had incredible authority. They even questioned Jesus about where His authority came from. The people of Israel had heard of such things in the past, but it had been hundreds of years since anything like this had taken place. Jesus genuinely amazed them.

The Gospel record includes many stories and statements related to Jesus' authority. It is possible to identify five different ways in which He exercised that authority in His ministry: teaching and preaching, healing, forgiving sins, deliverance, and power over creation.

The Sermon on the Mount has always been seen as one of the greatest teachings of all time. The people who listened to Jesus that day were no less impressed. Matthew records their reaction in chapter 7 of his Gospel. He wrote that when Jesus finished speaking they were amazed at His teaching because of the authority of His words. There was an obvious power behind what Jesus said to them, unlike, according to them, the teachings of the religious leaders of their day (Matthew 7:28–29). I am sure that the authority of Christ's words grew out of the anointing of the Holy Spirit. On another occasion, when Jesus taught in the synagogue of Capernaum, people reacted with the same amazement. His authority was unquestionable and unequalled.

Jesus also exercised the authority of God to heal people. He was clearly concerned and compassionate about individuals who were suffering physically. He demonstrated that the power of God was greater than disease by freeing people from the most debilitating infirmities. He healed many from leprosy, blindness, deafness, and the inability to speak. Jesus cured the woman with the hemorrhage of blood, the paralytic, the servant of the Roman centurion, and even raised Jairus' daughter from the dead. The man at the pool of Bethesda was healed from a disease that had infirmed him for thirty-eight years, and Lazarus was brought back to life after being entombed for three days. When Jesus spoke, even diseases surrendered to His authority.

There are several instances when Jesus exercised authority over creation. Once, Jesus sent His disciples ahead into the village of Bethsaida. He then went off alone to spend some time on the mountainside in prayer. When evening came the disciples were already in the middle of the lake straining at the oars because of the wind. Jesus simply walked across the water to meet them. They were so shocked they thought He was a ghost. Mark records that He just climbed into the boat and sat down, leaving the disciples completely amazed (Mark 6:45–52). That was neither the first nor last time Jesus did such things. He turned water into wine, brought fishes from an empty sea, turned five loaves and two fishes into a banquet, cursed a fig tree, and calmed an angry sea with a command. Each time the disciples were stunned by His authority. As they said, *"Even the wind and the waves obey him!"* (Mark 4:41).

Jesus also exercised authority over demons. Probably the most memorable account of deliverance in Jesus' ministry came in the region of the Gerasenes, where there was a man who had lived for years in a cemetery. He was greatly tormented by demons and had often been chained by the citizens of the area. But he would break loose and return to the tombs where he went about naked and mad. One day Jesus arrived and the man ran to Jesus and fell at His feet. The demonic powers that possessed him began to cry out, *"What do you want with me, Jesus, Son of the Most High God?"* (see Luke 8:26–39).

Jesus asked the demonic spirit what his name was, and he replied, "Legion," signifying that there were many demons in the man. The evil spirits begged Jesus not to order them into the Abyss. They knew He had the authority to do so. Jesus told the demons to enter a herd of pigs that were grazing in the area. When He did, the pigs went mad, rushing down the hillside into the sea, where they drowned. The man had been set free by the command of Christ. He wanted to follow Jesus, but the Lord told Him to go home and tell people what God had done for him. The local people were so stunned by Christ's authority that they asked Him to leave the region because they were overcome with fear.

Jesus confronted demons regularly in His ministry and they always submitted to His authority. They knew that He walked in the power of the Holy Spirit and had the God-given right to command them to go wherever He instructed. This too amazed people and caused them to seek Jesus out for healing and deliverance. Jesus said that He drove out demons by the finger of God, proof positive that the Kingdom of God had come to them (Luke 11:20).

Once while Jesus was visiting His home town, some men brought a paralyzed man to Him in hopes that He would heal him (Matthew 9:1–8). Jesus saw that these men had great faith and so He looked at the paralytic and said, *"Take heart, son; your sins are forgiven."* This statement infuriated the religious leaders who were there. They accused Jesus of blasphemy. Jesus then turned to them and said,

> *"'Why do you entertain evil thoughts in your hearts? Which is easier: to say, "Your sins are forgiven," or to say, "Get up and walk"? But so that you may know that the Son of Man has authority on earth to forgive sins . . .' Then he said to the paralytic, 'Get up, take your mat and go home.'"*
>
> (Matthew 9:4–6)

That is precisely what the man did. The people were overwhelmed with emotion and began to praise the Lord. Jesus had proven that He even had the authority to speak forgiveness over individuals, something that they had never seen before that day.

Jesus walked in the authority of God. All creation responded to His command, and as a result people were set free from the bondage of evil. They were no longer helpless before the strategies of the evil one, for the Kingdom of God had broken through in the person of Jesus Christ. The cross would assure the ultimate victory, as Jesus made a public display of Satan and all his evil schemes. There He disarmed their power and took away their authority. Jesus was the Christus Victor (Colossians 2:13–15).

Authority and the Followers of Christ

If asked, many Christians would say that Jesus walked in this incredible authority because He was God. But Scripture is quite clear about the fact that Jesus laid aside His divine glory in order to experience life as a human being (Philippians 2:6–8). What He did on earth was accomplished in His humanity, not His divinity. Undoubtedly Jesus' authority grew out of His relationship with the Heavenly Father, particularly the depth of intimacy that He experienced with God. But He ministered as a man who was in perfect harmony with the Father, moving with power and authority.

This can easily be supported by looking to the Gospels. Jesus did not keep the power and authority to Himself. He shared it with His followers, sending them into the world to minister as He was ministering. Matthew wrote of this in his Gospel. He said that Jesus specifically gave His followers the authority to drive out evil spirits and to heal every disease and sickness. He went on to give specific instructions to them, including:

> *"Do not go among the Gentiles or enter any town of the Samaritans. Go rather to the lost sheep of Israel. As you go, preach this message: 'The kingdom of heaven is near.' Heal the sick, raise the dead, cleanse those who have leprosy, drive out demons. Freely you have received, freely give."*
>
> (Matthew 10:5–8)

The disciples were certainly human beings. They had already proven that they did not understand everything about Christ and His ministry. Yet Jesus gave them authority over evil spirits and disease, proving that everyday Christians could minister as He did.

Luke tells the story of Jesus sending out seventy-two followers, two by two, into the towns and villages of the area. He wrote that they returned from their mission full of joy. They told Jesus that *"even the demons submit to us in your name.''* The scripture says that Jesus was full of joy through the Holy Spirit. He declared:

> *"I saw Satan fall like lightning from heaven. I have given you authority to trample on snakes and scorpions and to overcome all the power of the enemy; nothing will harm you. However, do not rejoice that the spirits submit to you, but rejoice that your names are written in heaven.''*
>
> (Luke 10:18–20)

The followers of Christ were given authority and power over the forces of darkness. They were thrilled, yet reminded by Jesus that their salvation was a far greater gift than being able to minister as He did.

Several times Jesus told His disciples that they could ask anything in His name and He would do it (Matthew 7:7; John 14:14; 16:24). Naturally this does not mean that Christians could ask to rob a bank and not get caught, or touch rocks and turn them into gold. The phrase *"in my name"* is critical to understanding this promise. Jesus was saying that disciples could move with His power and authority when doing things that He would do. When ministering *as* Jesus would, believers can have power and authority *like* Jesus exercised. There is absolutely no evidence that this promise was restricted to spiritual superstars. Ministering in power and authority is possible for every person who has the seed of Christ's nature within.

Why Are People No Longer Amazed?

In response to this truth certain questions beg to be asked: Why don't Christians minister with this authority today? Why are people no longer amazed when believers preach, and teach, and minister to the sick and dying? Why does

Christianity appear to be so powerless? The easy answer is that most Christians are spiritually immature. They do not minister as Jesus did because they are not growing to be more and more like Him. More specifically, I believe it is because of several identifiable issues. The first is a problem of world-view.

Most Christians in our society have been schooled to look at the world through the eyes of the Enlightenment. As such, the supernatural and spiritual dimensions of life are filtered out or explained away. The idea of demons and evil spirits is ridiculed, seen as unscientific beliefs of a less informed time. Evidence that would point to the demonic is explained away and, as a result, never addressed within the church. What results is a free reign for the forces of darkness to oppress and afflict people, both within and outside of the local church.

Second, many Christians do not know about the power and authority they have. They walk around as defenseless victims, all the while having the power and authority to push the enemy back in their own lives and also help others find freedom in Christ. I have prayed with countless believers who were being beat up by evil forces. I usually talk to them about the authority they have in Christ, and then help them pray for freedom. More often than not they are amazed at the authority they possess as believers. They can hardly believe that, like the disciples, they have both the power and authority to cast out demons, preach the gospel, and heal the sick in Jesus' name. Granted, doing this takes instruction, maturity, and discernment. But, under the guidance of mature Christian leaders, everyday believers can seriously impact the world in Jesus' name.

Third, many Christians are simply afraid of ministering with power and authority. They seem to hold a dualistic view of the universe, believing that Satan and God are two equal powers warring for the souls of human beings. That is not true. God is sovereign, all-powerful, and all-knowing. He is infinite, eternal, and Lord over all creation. Satan is a created being with limited power, already assigned a place in the lake of fire at the end of the age. Jesus defeated him at Calvary and ever since Satan has been on a short leash. Christians have been given power and authority in Christ and should minister with confidence, trusting that Satan is powerless in the presence of Christ's power, authority, and blood.

Fourth, Christians fail to exercise authority because they are not fully aware of their position in Christ. Ask believers where Jesus is today and they will say at the right hand of God. They would be right. Jesus is now in the place of all authority, Lord over all creation. But few Christians know that they are seated there with Him in the heavenly realms. Paul said that God has raised us up with Christ and seated us beside Him in heaven (Ephesians 2:6). Not only is Jesus in us, we are spiritually in Him, secured in a place of safety and authority.

I have learned to actually state out loud that I am seated with Christ before I pray for people. I do that for me, for those I am ministering to, and as a statement of faith in the face of darkness. I know that Jesus has, by grace, given me an authority that can be used to set the captives free. I want to grow to understand and operate in that authority as a mature follower of Christ.

Nourishment and Nurture

You are seated with Christ right now, secure in a position of power and authority. That is true because you have received Christ into your life as Savior and Lord, and been adopted as a child of God. All heaven knows that you have this authority. So do the forces of darkness, who hope that you never realize your full potential as a follower of Christ. What is important is that you recognize your position in Christ and allow the Holy Spirit to transform you into a spiritually mature believer who reflects the glory of Jesus Christ. This is the call of Jesus upon your life.

There are several ways in which you can position yourself to mature in the use of authority and power. First, always invest in your relationship with Christ. Authority and power in the spiritual realm are relationally based. That means that your devotional walk with the Lord is critical to ministering as He did. Jesus once warned people that many would prophesy, cast out demons, and work miracles in His name. But in the end He would separate Himself from them, because He did not know them (Matthew 7:21–23). As discussed in chapter 3, intimacy is a priority for growing Christians. There is transforming power in the Lord's presence which enables the seed of His nature to grow and flourish. Be faithful about spending time with the Lord.

Second, exercising the authority that you have in Christ demands that you be responsible as a mature Christian. Spiritual authority is given for the purpose of setting captive people free. It is not meant to be a sign of your worth, proof that you are important, or a power that is to be used in a cavalier manner. Peter once came across a sorcerer who wanted to buy spiritual authority from him, as though it were some kind of magic. Peter rebuked the man, telling him that his heart was not right and that he needed to repent of his self-serving attitude (Acts 8:9–25). You should understand that exercising spiritual power and authority requires that you grow and learn as a faithful minister of the Lord. There are definitely right and wrong ways to minister to people.

In my experience people find it helpful when they can be mentored in the essentials of ministry by a mature believer. Jesus did this with the disciples and the seventy-two. He laid out a series of principles that helped them exercise authority in a responsible and effective way (Matthew 10:1–42; Luke 10:1–22). Mentoring is a biblically sound approach to instruction and helps less mature Christians learn about ministering with authority in a safe environment. I would also encourage you to read *I Give You Authority* by Charles Kraft (Chosen Books, 1997). His book is a thorough treatment on Christians and authority, based primarily on the testimony of Scripture.

Third, be sure that you are ministering in accountability to other believers. When Paul decided to begin his ministry to the Gentiles he traveled to Jerusalem to meet with the Apostles. He wanted to be sure that he was serving Christ in line with sound teaching and practice (Galatians 2:1–2). Peter did similarly when he went to minister to Cornelius, a Gentile from Caesarea (Acts 11:1 18). The early disciples clearly walked in the authority and power of the Lord. They worked incredible signs and wonders and regularly set people free from demonic bondage. But, they were no lone rangers. They knew that Christians needed to be accountable to each other under the Lordship of Christ. Isolation in ministry can lead to deception and imbalance. The body of Christ is to be a united fellowship where men and women willingly submit themselves to one another. You would do well to be closely connected to other mature believers as you step out to minister in the authority that is yours in Christ.

Fourth, remember that Jesus calls you to minister in the spirit of humility. Jesus humbled Himself in ministry, even though He walked in incredible power and authority. He emptied Himself of all glory so as to touch the least and weakest, even kneeling to wash the feet of the disciples. The attitude of Christ should be shared by all believers, regardless of the manifestation of God's power in their ministry.

Power and authority can be seductive even among the people of God. More than once, gifted spiritual leaders have fallen because they began to take themselves too seriously. They began to act as though they were better and more important than others because God powerfully used them. Paul sounded a clear warning about this when he wrote,

> *"Do nothing out of selfish ambition or vain conceit, but in humility consider others better than yourselves."*
> (Philippians 2:3)

The authority you have is given as a gift of grace. Hold that gift lightly, remembering that it flows from the very throne room of God.

Jesus Christ amazed people by the way He ministered with authority and power. He did everything the prophet Isaiah predicted, preaching good news to the poor, bringing freedom to the captives, healing the blind, and releasing the oppressed (Isaiah 61:1–2). The Spirit of the Lord had anointed Him with the authority of the Kingdom, and people were changed forever. Demons and darkness were subject to His commands, and even the wind and the waves obeyed Him.

Jesus calls you to be like Him. That does not mean that you will work the same signs and wonders that Jesus did. But you *can* minister in the authority of the Kingdom. You do have the power and right to set people free from the forces of darkness. God has given you that as a follower of His Son. Even now you are seated with Christ in the heavenlies, which secures you in a place of incredible authority. His nature is already at work within you, which enables you to become more and more like Jesus. Allow the Holy Spirit access to your life. He will nourish and nurture you, helping you to grow into a spiritually mature disciple of Jesus.

Chapter 10

Setting Priorities

In the mid 1960s the Christian community was becoming increasingly aware of a man named David Wilkerson. His story about street preaching to violent gangs in New York City was receiving national attention, and was eventually made into a book and motion picture entitled *The Cross and the Switchblade*. I was a teenager at the time and had only an occasional relationship with the local church. But some Christians from my area chartered a bus to hear David Wilkerson speak at a Kathryn Kuhlman meeting in Pittsburgh. I knew a lot of the teens who were going, so I tagged along, little knowing what was about to happen to me.

The meeting was held in the Pittsburgh Syria Mosque, which was filled to capacity that night. I sat in the middle section of the second balcony, looking directly down on the stage. Several members of New York City street gangs had come with David Wilkerson and were seated beside him on the platform. I remember staring, wondering if life for them was anything like the movie *West Side Story*. Kathryn Kuhlman was holding the rally, so she welcomed everyone and introduced the speaker.

Wilkerson talked about his ministry in New York and introduced the gang members, who had been converted to Christ. His stories about threats and confrontations with them caught my interest. He then began to preach. I was pretty much prepared to check out mentally when he began, but his words held incredible power. Even after thirty-five years I remember that his theme was "The Sword of the Lord." He talked about God coming in judgment and how people needed to be saved. A growing sense of fear grabbed me as he spoke, so much so that I got out of my seat and went into the restroom, hoping to get away from what he was saying. But there were speakers in the bathrooms and I still could hear him preaching. I was so worked up that I wanted to leave, but the bus was my only way home. I went back to my seat, hoping that it would not last much longer.

As I sat there, the conviction of the Lord was weighing heavily upon me. When David Wilkerson ended his sermon, he invited people to come forward and be saved by Jesus. At first I tried to resist. But soon I found myself up front, kneeling beneath the platform. There were hundreds of people at the front, so a man came and led several of us up on stage in order to give other people room to respond. We were invited to kneel, which I did, right in front of a man named Nicki Cruz. In broken English he led me in a prayer to receive the Lord. I was crying more deeply than I had ever done before. What began as tears of fear somewhere changed to deep joy, for something real had taken place inside of me.

Unexpectedly Kathryn Kuhlman came over and led me to the microphone. She asked me to tell the crowd what had happened to me. Through tears I said that I had accepted Jesus into my heart. People applauded and Kathryn prayed for me. She then said, "Young man, someday you are going to serve the Lord." With that I went back to my friends and the eventual bus ride home. The people I went with seemed very happy for me, which helped me feel less anxious about everything that had happened. I ended up becoming a part of a youth group and tried to be a good follower of Christ.

But the truth is, very little changed in my life as a result of that night. The touch from the Lord was genuine. But I did not allow it to go deep into my life. I ran with the same friends, rebelled in the same ways, and was committed to not being all that serious about the whole thing. My school buddies had no idea about what had happened. I was embarrassed and afraid they would make fun of me, so I didn't tell them. I convinced myself that being saved was a private thing, so keeping it mostly to myself was fine. But in a very short time all evidence that I was a Christian was gone, and for the next seven or eight years I did not walk with the Lord. Ultimately, it was the love of some college friends that led me to surrender my life fully to Christ, and true change began to happen.

I did not share this story with anyone for many years. I have only recently recognized that it was a very important event in my life, particularly the prayer of Kathryn Kuhlman. I believe that some level of anointing was placed upon me that night, which lay dormant for years because I had not taken my relationship with the Lord seriously. The Lord was working to draw me to Himself, but I resisted making the level of commitment necessary to truly grow as His disciple. That significantly hurt my spiritual life, causing me to languish in immaturity and inconsistency, when I could have been becoming more like Jesus.

Becoming Like Jesus Demands Serious Commitment

This book has been about becoming like Jesus. Christians are called to be increasingly transformed into His likeness, the true mark of spiritual maturity. Eight characteristics of Jesus Christ have been discussed, each presented as qualities that believers are to share with the Lord. Those characteristics are defined as follows:

The Characteristics of Christ

- Jesus rooted His identity in His position as God's Beloved Son
- Jesus experienced intimacy with the Heavenly Father
- Jesus was committed to community as a context for growth and ministry
- Jesus prioritized character above behavior
- Jesus responded properly to personal brokenness
- Jesus offered His wounds as a source of ministry to others
- Jesus was empowered in life by the Holy Spirit
- Jesus ministered with Kingdom authority

These characteristics are part of the nature of Christ that is present within believers from the day they are born again, but it takes the transforming work of the Holy Spirit to nourish and nurture them toward spiritual maturity. That process demands a high level of commitment from Christians. If the seed of Christ's nature is ignored, immaturity is the result. That is what happened in my life following my encounter with God at the Wilkerson rally.

Becoming like Jesus does not just happen. People who are serious about the call of Christ must make commitments that position them for the Spirit's transforming touch. These commitments do not in themselves bring change, but they do make room for the Holy Spirit to work in believers' lives. Spiritual maturity demands a level of devotion and consecration that is simply not made by many Christians, even by those in leadership. As a result, the Church is struggling in a crisis of immaturity. Even Jesus Christ lived His life in a way that made space for God's nourishing and nurturing presence.

Establishing Priorities

Each of the chapters has ended with several practical suggestions that will help you experience the transforming work of the Holy Spirit. But it will take serious attention on your part to turn those into realities in your life. Time and resources must be rearranged, making room for personal growth and development. Granted, the Holy Spirit will use all of life as the context for spiritual maturation, but you must devote very specific amounts of time and resource to that ongoing process.

I have been a Christian for three decades, and I know that there is always something that demands my attention, often masquerading as some dire emergency. For years the tyranny of the urgent seemed to control all the resources of my life. As a result, I had little room for devotional intimacy, had only shallow commitments to community, and was totally ignoring the deep emotional wounds that were compromising my life. I was caught in a crisis of immaturity and breakdown resulted.

Many Christians are caught in that same destructive pattern. I spend a considerable amount of time teaching spiritual formation to pastors and other Christian leaders. Almost every one of them admits that their priorities are way out of balance. They have a genuine internal desire to be closer to the Lord and to experience personal growth and wellbeing, but they allow the demands of ministry to determine how they spend their time. Invariably personal devotional disciplines are squeezed from their lives. Eventually their spiritual capital is depleted, and their ministries become increasingly ineffective. Even then it is difficult for them to make the changes that will benefit their own spiritual development. As a result they are locked in immaturity.

Growing in the eight characteristics of Christ will not simply happen spontaneously. You must give attention to each under the guidance of the Holy Spirit. I encourage you to look at your schedule and make room for your spiritual growth. In all likelihood you will need to eliminate in order to concentrate. You will need to learn to say no to some things in order to say yes to God. Remember, that does not mean that you are to be tirelessly doing ministry and going to church every night of the week. Spiritual maturation demands far more wisdom than that.

Establishing priorities means that you are making room for spiritual growth. You should schedule time to enter the presence of the Lord, grow as His child, and experience the healing power of His presence. Many of the characteristics are best developed in genuine Christian community. That means that you will need to find a group of people who will grow with you, teach you about ministry, pray for the healing of your wounds, and position you for the infilling of the Holy Spirit. This all demands time at two levels: you must give time and spiritual maturation takes time.

Even a cursory reading of the Gospels shows that Jesus lived according to certain priorities. While He came to earth with a clear mission, He did not allow the demands of ministry to determine how He spent His time. No matter how much people pushed, Jesus would get away to be alone with His Father. He also was committed to spending time with His community. I am always amazed at the fact that Jesus did not even begin His active ministry until He was thirty years old. I am convinced that the unknown years of His life were dedicated to personal growth and development. We would do well to follow His example.

Making commitments to grow in Christ is not an easy process. You are most likely a busy person with many demands being placed upon you. But there are some changes that you cannot afford not to make. I encourage you to review the practical suggestions that are made at the end of each chapter. Ask the Lord to help you identify where and how to begin investing in your spiritual growth. Most likely you are already being attentive to several of these issues. But there are probably some characteristics of Christ that need to be prioritized. Allow the Holy Spirit to quicken you as to the specific areas where He desires to be active in your life. Make your deepest investments there.

The Starting Place

I am convinced that the first three characteristics discussed in this book are foundational to growing in the remainder of them. Be sure that they are in place as you seek to grow and develop. First, learn about who you are in Christ Jesus. So much of the Christian life is related to that issue. It holds the key to your personal wellbeing and confidence in life. Stay positioned before the Holy Spirit in that area of your development, for it is critical to spiritual maturity.

Second, spend time developing intimacy with the Lord. Embrace a lifestyle that enables you to give time, space, and spiritual disciplines to the Lord. If you do, the Holy Spirit will draw you into the loving arms of the Father. Third, commit to your spiritual community. Having a place to grow with other believers is vital. Remember that Jesus Himself promised to be there, when even two or three of you meet in His name. With these three commitments in place, you will be able to grow and develop into the person God intended you to be.

Conclusion

Jesus never sugar-coated the call to become His disciple. He told the disciples that those who choose to follow Him must deny themselves, pick up the cross, and follow where He leads. He then said,

> *"... whoever wants to save his life will lose it, but whoever loses his life for me will find it."* (Matthew 16:25)

There are those today who think that being a Christian demands little more than asking to be saved. It means saying a simple four-point prayer and then carrying a decision card around in their purse or wallet. They have somewhere learned a form of easy believe-ism that may be attractive, but is ultimately powerless and certainly unbiblical.

Jesus wants you to become like Him. That demands laying down life as you know it, to embrace life as Jesus lived it. He does not ask you to do this in your own strength or ability. He placed the seed of His nature within you to make Christ-likeness possible. Jesus has also given you the Holy Spirit to lead and empower the process of change. All that is needed now is you, surrendered and willing. The call to become like Jesus is clear. Will you say yes to this glorious invitation and experience a transformed life?

If you have enjoyed this book and would like to help us to send a copy of it and many other titles to needy pastors in the **Third World**, please write for further information or send your gift to:

**Sovereign World Trust
PO Box 777, Tonbridge
Kent TN11 0ZS
United Kingdom**

or to the '**Sovereign World**' distributor in your country.

Visit our website at **www.sovereign-world.org**
for a full range of Sovereign World books.